Irene C. Fountas & Gay Su Pinnell

Sing a Song of
Poetry

Cassandra Biette

Cassandra Biette

Irene C. Fountas & Gay Su Pinnell

Sing a Song of
Poetry

A Teaching Resource for Phonemic Awareness, Phonics, and Fluency

Kindergarten

Revised Edition

HEINEMANN
Portsmouth, NH

Heinemann

361 Hanover Street

Portsmouth, NH 03801–3912

www.heinemann.com

Offices and agents throughout the world

Cataloging-in-Publication Data is on file at the Library of Congress.

ISBN-13: 978-0-325-09291-1

Previously published under ISBN-13: 978-0-325-00655-0

Editorial: Kimberly Capriola, David Pence
Production: Hilary Goff
Cover and interior designs: Monica Ann Crigler
Typesetter: Gina Poirier Design
Manufacturing: Erin St. Hilaire

Printed in the United States of America on acid-free paper

22 21 20 19 18 VP 1 2 3 4 5

Contents

Poems

A

B

Contents

H

I

Contents

M

O

Introduction

Sing a Song of Poetry rolls off the tongue and moves the heart and spirit, if not the feet and hands. Rhythmical language of any sort delights young children as it surrounds them with the magical sounds of dancing words. But poetry, verse, and song provide the magic of teaching as well; indeed, oral language is the doorway to the world of written language and the foundation for literacy. As kindergartners respond to the sound patterns, intriguing words, and inspiring ideas they find in poems, songs, and rhymes, they are learning invaluable lessons about the ways in which our language works—knowledge that will serve them well as they become readers and writers.

The poems, songs, and rhymes in this volume are a rich source of language, ideas, and imagery that will help kindergarten children use and enjoy oral and written language. This volume is a companion to the lessons described in *The Fountas & Pinnell Phonics, Spelling, and Word Study Lessons, Kindergarten* (2018). It can also be used as a stand-alone resource for language and literacy opportunities in any early childhood or primary classroom.

Jack, be nimble,
Jack be quick,
Jack, jump over
The candlestick.

A poem illustrated by a child in an Apply activity in a kindergarten classroom

Experiences with poetry help children become aware of the phonological system of language and provide a foundation for matching sounds with letters, letter clusters, and word parts. You can use poems, chants, and songs to help children

- listen for and identify rhyming words;
- connect words that have the same beginning, ending, or medial sound;
- begin to match sounds to letters in words;
- introduce the culture, traditional language, and rhythmic patterns of nursery rhymes;
- stimulate and enrich language development;
- promote phonemic awareness by helping them notice words; syllables; rhymes; onsets and rimes; and beginning, ending, and medial sounds;
- enhance oral language use in articulate ways;
- instill an appreciation of poetry and prose;
- build vocabulary;
- experience meaningful print and learn early reading behaviors (e.g., directionality, word by word matching);
- participate in fluent, phrased reading;
- build meaningful concepts about print (letters, words, punctuation);
- introduce letters and set the scene for letter recognition; and
- provide a base from which to explore writing.

Once a poem is introduced in your classroom, it has multiple uses for teaching. Below are some examples.

- Reread the poem to have children highlight rhyming words with highlighter tape.
- Reread the poem with sticky notes over rhyming words so children can predict.
- Cover all but the first letter of several words, and have children predict and then check them as you reread.
- Have children highlight any features of words that they are studying: e.g., first letters, onsets, rimes, and endings.
- Cover names in the poem with sticky notes and substitute with children's names.
- Give children a small version of the poem that they can glue in a personal poetry book and then illustrate.
- During independent work time, let children read their personal poetry book with a partner.
- During independent work time, children can read the chart with a partner.

In addition to activities like those above, read the suggestions in small print at the bottom of each poem. They describe ways you can work with the poem— sometimes adding verses or changing them.

Young children love poetry with rhythm and rhyme; the language of poetry sings inside their heads. As they grow older, they will learn to appreciate poetry without rhyme, but rhymes and songs are the staple of early childhood and for good reason.

Sing a Song of Poetry, Kindergarten

Values and Goals of Poetry in Kindergarten Classrooms

Poetry expands children's oral language abilities as it:

- provides texts that are easy to remember;
- builds a repertoire of the unique patterns and forms of language;
- helps children become sensitive to and enjoy the sounds of language–rhymes, alliteration, assonance, onomatopoeia (buzz, whiz, woof);
- supports articulation and elocution;
- extends listening and speaking vocabularies;
- expands knowledge of the complex syntax of language;
- encourages children to manipulate and play with language;
- develops phonological awareness (rhyme, syllables, onsets, and rimes);
- makes it easy for children to isolate and identify sounds, take words apart, change sounds in words to make new words;
- develops phonemic awareness (the ability to manipulate individual sounds); and
- provides rich examples of comparisons such as similes and metaphors.

Poetry expands children's written language abilities as it:

- gives them access to memorable language that they can then match up with print;
- expands spoken vocabulary, making it easier later for them to read words;
- helps them notice aspects of print;
- provides opportunities to learn and recognize words that rhyme, end the same, start the same, or sound the same in the middle;
- helps them begin to notice the letters and letter patterns associated with sounds;
- provides a setting in which to develop the concept of a word and notice how spaces are used to define words in written language; and
- provides models of fluent reading to help children get the feel of it.

Poetry expands children's content knowledge as it:

- provides new perceptions and ideas for them to think about;
- helps them develop conceptual understandings;
- encourages them to develop a sense of humor; and
- sensitizes them to the forms and styles of poetry.

Poetry contributes to children's social knowledge and skills as it:

- provides artistic and aesthetic experiences;
- creates a sense of community through enjoying rhymes and songs as a group;
- gives them access to English-speaking culture;
- provides a window to many other cultures;
- provides a common language for a group of children to share; and
- creates memories of shared enjoyable times.

Often rhymes, chants, and songs contain *onomatopoeia*, which is the representation of sound with words. For example, words like *whoosh* sound like the phenomenon they represent. Consider this example or a different verse from "The Wheels on the Bus":

> The wipers on the bus
>
> Go swish, swish, swish,
>
> Swish, swish, swish,
>
> Swish, swish, swish.
>
> The wipers on the bus
>
> Go swish, swish, swish
>
> All around the town.

Poetry often presents children with verses that have been enjoyed for centuries. Sometimes they can internalize archaic language like *porridge* and *candlestick* as they chant and sing. But some archaic concepts may warrant explanation: e.g., *Down with the lambs* and *Up with the lark* in the poem "Bedtime," or roosters crowing as an alarm clock. Additionally, old-fashioned language structures and expressions like *art thou* in the poem "Bow-Wow-Wow" may need to be defined. They are often—though not solely—present in nursery rhymes.

Language Patterns

Rhymes and poems are enjoyable in large part because of the language patterns that are included. *Alliteration*, the repetition of consonant sounds, is evident in this familiar nursery rhyme, "Georgy Porgy":

> Georgy Porgy, pudding and pie,
>
> Kissed the girls and made them cry.
>
> When the boys came out to play,
>
> Georgy Porgy ran away.

Another common pattern is the repetition of vowel sounds, called *assonance*. The familiar poem, "Jack Sprat," repeats the short *a* sound and the long *e* sound.

> Jack Sprat could eat no fat.
>
> His wife could eat no lean.
>
> And so between them both, you see,
>
> They licked the platter clean.

Repetition

Many poems, particularly songs, have repeating stanzas or phrases. Notice that in the following familiar nursery rhyme, "Pease Porridge Hot," *hot, cold*; *in the pot*; and *nine days old* are all repeated.

> Pease porridge hot,
>
> Pease porridge cold,
>
> Pease porridge in the pot,
>
> Nine days old.
>
> Some like it hot,
>
> Some like it cold,
>
> Some like it in the pot,
>
> Nine days old.

Rhythmic repetition like this helps children learn these rhymes easily; many have been set to music and can be sung, such as the poem "The Muffin Man."

Sensory Images

Poetry arouses the senses. Just a few words can evoke memories, elicit visual images, point out absurdities, and help us enter unique worlds. Many children feel they have met the lady in the nursery rhyme "Ride a Cockhorse to Banbury Cross":

> Ride a cockhorse
>
> To Banbury Cross,
>
> To see a fine lady
>
> Upon a white horse;
>
> Rings on her fingers
>
> And bells on her toes,
>
> She shall have music
>
> Wherever she goes.

Important Areas of Learning for Kindergarten Children

The most important benefit of using poetry in kindergarten classrooms is the facilitation of children's oral language development. Through their involvement in poetry, children expand their knowledge of the vocabulary and syntax of English as well as their sensitivity to the phonology or sounds of the language. In addition, using poetry has profound implications for helping children learn to read and write. See *Guided Reading: Responsive Teaching Across the Grades*, Second Edition (Fountas and Pinnell, 2017) and *Word Matters: Teaching Phonics and Spelling in the Reading/Writing Classroom* (Pinnell and Fountas, 1998).

Several important areas of learning form a foundation for becoming literate. Even though formal reading instruction would not occur until the second half of kindergarten, young children need to develop along all of these dimensions through the early childhood years.

Phonological Awareness

The phonological system encompasses the sounds of a language. When children hear, chant, or sing poems, they become more aware of sound patterns and how they are connected (for example, words that rhyme or words that start the same). Gradually, they are able to identify the individual sounds (or *phonemes*) in words. *Phonemic awareness*, or the ability to identify individual sounds in words, is essential when children are learning to connect sounds and letters. Young children need to learn to play with language and manipulate sounds. They can

- listen for and identify rhyming words;
- listen for and identify syllables within words;
- listen for and identify onsets and rimes;
- listen for individual sounds in words;
- match words with similar sounds;
- break words into individual sounds (phonemes) and into syllables;
- blend sounds to form words; and
- match sounds and letters.

Letter Learning

To be able to recognize letters, children need to distinguish the features that make one letter different from every other letter. The differences between letters are sometimes quite small (for example, *h* and *n*), and distinguishing such features requires close attention. Also, orientation makes a difference (for example, *u* and *n*). Learning how to look at letters is essential if children are to connect sounds and letters and and learn letter names. Through repeated exposure to letters in the poems they experience in shared reading, children begin to notice the letters that are embedded in print. They can

> ▶ notice and locate letters in words;
> ▶ learn to find the beginning letter of a word;
> ▶ connect words by beginning or ending letters; and
> ▶ connect words in poems to letters in their names.

Phonics

Teaching children how the sounds of language are connected to the letters (to learn letter-sound relationships) is an instructional approach called *phonics*. Early on, young children will learn the easy-to-hear consonant sounds (beginning or ending) and easy-to-hear vowels (long vowels).

Concepts About Print

Encounters with poetry will also help children acquire some basic understandings about how print works. For example, the concepts of first and last are important in written language. Children who are just beginning to notice the world of print will have the opportunity to learn that they read from left to right across a line of print and that at the end of the line, you return to the left and again read left to right. One spoken word matches one group of printed letters, and a printed word has a space on each side of it. It is important for children to understand that letters are embedded in print and that they can identify words by the sequence of the letters. They can

> ▶ notice print as the carrier of the message in a text;
> ▶ follow print from top to bottom and over pages of text;
> ▶ follow print left to right in a familiar text;
> ▶ return to the left margin at the end of the line;
> ▶ locate words by saying them and thinking about the first sound and letter;
> ▶ find rhyming words;
> ▶ recognize upper and lower case letters;
> ▶ locate letters and familiar words in text;
> ▶ distinguish between a letter and a word; and
> ▶ notice simple punctuation.

Fluency

Young children will become verbally fluent as they repeat poems and use the phrases, pauses, stresses, and intonation of the language. They will also become more fluent in picking up the print from the page as many words become more automatic and their reading vocabulary expands. They can

- read in phrases;
- use expression;
- stop at periods and pause at commas;
- raise the voice at question marks;
- sound excited at an exclamation mark;
- read smoothly;
- put their words together so it sounds like language;
- vary intonation and stress to reflect meaning; and
- recognize some words quickly.

Selecting Poetry for Young Children

Selecting poetry for children depends on your purpose. You will want to consider whether they will experience the poems orally or if you will eventually expect them to process the print. Children can listen to and recite more complex poems than they can read. Simple, engaging, repetitive poems will be easy for them to remember. Knowing poems, songs, and rhymes increases children's ability to notice the sounds of language; they learn many new words to add to their oral vocabulary. When they repeat familiar poems, they are using the syntax, or grammar, of written language, which is different from their everyday speech. Experiencing and internalizing this complex language sets the scene for reading and understanding the simple texts they will begin to read as well as the more complex texts they will encounter later.

In shared reading, children will begin to read with you (using an enlarged version of the text that everyone can see). In the process, they will begin to notice characteristics of print. The first poems children encounter in shared reading should

- be relatively short;
- employ repetition and patterned language;
- feature a large number of words that are easy to read;
- present generally simple vocabulary (although children may enjoy many rhymes without knowing the precise meaning of some archaic words, such as *pease porridge*); and
- focus on concepts and ideas that are familiar (for example, visual imagery and metaphor require more of children than simple rhymes and songs).

We recommend that kindergarten children have the opportunity to read a large number of poems in this highly supported way. The poems in this book represent a gradient of difficulty. At the beginning of the year, select very simple poems, and then gradually increase the level of challenge. The poems in the chart below illustrate a continuum of difficulty.

1. Simplest

I Love Chocolate

I love chocolate

Yum, yum, yum.

I love chocolate

In my tum.

2. More Difficult

Hey Diddle Diddle

Hey diddle diddle,

The cat and the fiddle,

The cow jumped over the moon;

The little dog laughed

To see such sport,

And the dish ran away with the spoon.

3. Most Difficult

Twinkle, Twinkle, Little Star

Twinkle, twinkle, little star,

How I wonder what you are!

Up above the world so high,

Like a diamond in the sky.

Twinkle, twinkle, little star,

How I wonder what you are!

Verse 1 is both simple and short. The theme is easy, there are few syllables, and there is repetition. Children can say it over and over while substituting other foods. Verse 2 is a common nursery rhyme with longer lines. There is some nonsensical imagery, but it is easy to grasp and the rhythm helps children learn it. Verse 3, "Twinkle, Twinkle, Little Star," evokes sensory imagery and metaphor. This riddle requires thinking beyond the actual words.

As you select poems to share, consider your children's previous experience, skill with language, and vocabulary. If you begin with easy poems and they learn them very quickly (for example, they join in and can soon repeat them independently), provide slightly more complex examples.

Planning for Teaching Opportunities When Revisiting a Text

As short texts, poems provide a multitude of opportunities for learning about language. At first, you will be using the poems only to expand oral language, but the experience will give children plenty of chances to:

- ▶ use interesting language;
- ▶ say and connect words of one, two, and three syllables;
- ▶ say and connect words that rhyme or that begin alike;
- ▶ say words, noticing beginning and ending sounds of consonants; and
- ▶ say words, noticing vowel sounds.

After enjoying a poem several times, you may want to revisit the text with children to help them notice features of print such as letters, letter patterns, or words. The following grid helps you think about the varied opportunities in some sample texts. In each box, we list possible features that children can notice within a poem. You can try planning some poems out for yourself in advance or use the blank grid to keep a record of your teaching points within each poem as you make them.

WORD-ANALYSIS TEACHING OPPORTUNITIES WHEN REVISITING POETRY

Title	Type of Text (e.g., limerick, tongue twister, couplet, free verse)	Phonogram Patterns (e.g., -at, -ig, -ate, -ile)	Letter-Sound (e.g., beginning or ending consonants and consonant digraphs)	High-Frequency Words	Other (e.g., concept words like colors and numbers; names; plurals; rhyming words; syllables; new vocabulary)
I Love Chocolate	4–line poem with rhyme pair	-um	Beginning l, ch, y, m, t Ending t, m, v, n	I, in, my	three-syllable word, assonance (/ŭ/), food concept, repetitive word (yum), rhyming words (yum, tum)
Hey Diddle Diddle	nursery rhyme	-at, -ow, -an, -ay	Beginning h, d, th, c, f, j, m, l, t, s, r, w Ending y, l, t, d, w, r, n, g, ch	the, and, to, see, with	one- and two-syllable words, assonance (/o͞o/), -ed ending, action words (jumped, laughed, ran)
Twinkle, Twinkle, Little Star	nursery rhyme rhyming couplets 1st, 2nd, 5th, and 6th lines rhyme, and the 3rd and 4th lines rhyme	-ow, -at	Beginning t, l, s, h, w, y, d Ending l, r, w, t, p, d, k, n	I, what, you, up, the, like, a, in	one- and two-syllable words, new vocabulary (twinkle, star, wonder, world, diamond, sky)
Hot Cross Buns	nursery rhyme rhythmic chant	-ot, -un	Beginning h, b, t, y, n, d, g, s Ending t, s, f, v, m, r	you, have, no, to	multisyllable words, plural ending -s, repetition of lines, counting words
Pat-a-cake	nursery rhyme hand play strong rhythm	-an, -ake, -at, -ut, -en	Beginning p, b, m, c, f, y, w, th, t Ending k, n, t, n, d,	me, a, you, can, it, and, with, in, the, for	multisyllable words, alliteration (/p/), rhyming words (man, can; bake, cake)

Introduction

WORD-ANALYSIS TEACHING OPPORTUNITIES WHEN REVISITING POETRY

Title	Type of Text (e.g., limerick, tongue twister, couplet, free verse)	Phonogram Patterns (e.g., -at, -ig, -ate, -ile)	Letter-Sound (e.g., beginning or ending consonants and consonant digraphs)	High-Frequency Words	Other (e.g., concept words like colors and numbers; names; plurals; rhyming words; syllables; new vocabulary)

Tools for Using Poetry

The tools for working with poetry are simple. You will want to have them well organized and readily available for quick lessons. We suggest the following:

Easel

A vertical surface for displaying chart paper, or the pocket chart, that is large enough for all children to see and sturdy enough to avoid tipping

Pocket Chart

A stiff piece of cardboard or plastic that has lines with grooves into which cards can be inserted so that children can work with lines of poems and/or individual words

Masks

Cutout cardboard shapes designed to outline words on charts for children to use in locating words or parts of words (see templates in *Teacher Tools*)

Highlighter Tape

Transparent stick-on tape that can be used to emphasize words, letters, or word parts

Sticky Notes

Small pieces of paper that have a sticky backing and can temporarily be used to conceal words or parts of words so that children can attend to them

Flags

A handle with a flat piece of wood or cardboard on the end that can be placed under a word on a chart as a way to locate or emphasize it (see template in *Teacher Tools*)

Tags

Signs with concise directions so that children can remember an independent work activity; for example, *Read, Mix, Fix, Read* represents *Read* the poem, *Mix* up the sentence strips of a poem, *Fix* the poem back together, and *Read* it again to check it

Art Materials

Media such as paint, glue, colored paper, and tissue paper

Instructional Contexts for Poetry

Poetry fits well into the range of activities typical in kindergarten classrooms.

Interactive Read-Aloud

Reading aloud forms a foundation for language and literacy development, and much poetry is meant to be read orally. In addition, reading aloud provides a model of fluent, phrased reading. There are many wonderful picture books that present rhyming verse to children in a very engaging way. *The Eensy-Weensy Spider* (Hoberman and Westcott) is an illustrated variation of the familiar verse. Other engaging retellings or adaptations of nursery rhymes from the *Fountas & Pinnell Classroom™ Interactive Read-Aloud Collection, Kindergarten* (2018) include *Baa Baa Black Sheep* (Trapani 2001), *I'm a Little Teapot* (Trapani 1996), *It's Raining, It's Pouring* (Eagle 1994), and *This Is the House That Jack Built* (Adams 1977).

We recommend repeated readings of favorite poems or rhyming books; it takes many repetitions for children to be able to join in. Ask them to listen the first two or three times you read a verse, but encourage them to join in after they have grasped enough to say it with you, especially on a refrain. In this way, children will begin to internalize much of the language, enjoy it more, and also get the feeling of participating in fluent, phrased reading.

Shared Reading

Shared reading allows children to both hear the verse and see the print. It uses an enlarged text—a big book or a chart that you have prepared or purchased. Such a shared approach allows you to demonstrate pointing while reading. After one or two repetitions, encourage children to read with you in interactive read-aloud. Be sure that all children can see the visual display of print. You'll want to sit or stand to the side and use a thin pointer (pointers that have objects like balls or hands on the end usually block children's view of the very word you are pointing out). The idea is to maximize children's attention to the print. Shared reading helps them learn how the eyes work in reading. They'll also learn more about rhyme and rhythm.

Choral Reading and Performance

Choral reading is a more sophisticated version of shared reading. Participants may read from an enlarged text, but often they have their own individual copies. They may have a leader, but it is not always necessary for the leader to point to the words. Participants can practice reading together several times and then perform the piece. You can assign solo lines, boys' and girls' lines, question and response lines, or whole-group lines. If there is dialogue, you can assign roles. Emphasize varying the voice to suit the meaning of the poem. You can add sound effects (wooden sticks, bells, or other simple tools) or simply invite children to clap or snap their fingers to accentuate words or phrases. Children also love using hand motions.

Independent Reading

Children love reading poetry, searching for favorite poems, and illustrating poems. A personal poetry book or anthology becomes a treasure. After poems have been read in shared reading, you can reproduce them on smaller pieces of paper. Children glue the poems into a composition book or spiral notebook and illustrate them. Be sure that you are using poems that they are familiar with and can read. Reading their personal poetry books is a good independent reading activity. You'll want to use nursery rhymes and very simple poems for kindergarten children while also helping to guide the process.

Writing Poetry

Children can begin to get a feel for writing verse through interactive writing. In interactive writing, you and the children compose a message together. You act as a scribe, using the easel, but occasionally children come up and write in a word or letter when you want to draw attention to it. See *Interactive Writing: How Language and Literacy Come Together, K–2,* (McCarrier, Pinnell, and Fountas 2000).

You can substitute children's names in a verse or create a variation of one of their favorites (for example, for "I Love Chocolate," substitute chocolate for all of their favorite foods). This activity gives them power over language and may inspire children to experiment on their own.

Types of Poetry

Poetry can be categorized in many different ways: e.g., by pattern, structure, or topic. This book includes rhymes and poems under the headings discussed below, which are related to forms, literary features, and themes. Many of the poems could be placed in more than one category.

Nursery Rhymes

Traditional rhymes by anonymous poets have been passed down over generations. There are often many different versions. Originally serving as political satire for adults, they have been loved by children for generations. They usually rhyme in couplets or alternating lines and are highly rhythmic. Young children enjoy these simple verses, and nursery rhymes help to build a foundation that will later lead

them to a more sophisticated appreciation of poetry. The Mother Goose nursery rhymes, which were published in the eighteenth century, are the best known, but equivalents exist around the world. An example of a Mother Goose nursery rhyme that children love is "Humpty Dumpty":

> Humpty Dumpty sat on a wall,
>
> Humpty Dumpty had a great fall;
>
> All the king's horses and all the king's men,
>
> Couldn't put Humpty together again.

Rhymed Verse

Many poems for young children have lines that end with words that rhyme. These may be *rhyming couplets* (each pair of lines rhyme), as in the poem "Cobbler, Cobbler":

> Cobbler, cobbler, mend my shoe.
>
> Get it done by half past two;
>
> Stitch it up and stitch it down.
>
> Then I'll give you half a crown.

Or, every other line may rhyme, as in the poem "Peas":

> I eat my peas with honey,
>
> I've done it all my life.
>
> It makes the peas taste funny,
>
> But it keeps them on the knife.

There are a variety of other rhyming patterns such as in the poem "I Scream":

> I scream.
>
> You scream.
>
> We all scream
>
> For ice cream!

Free Verse (Unrhymed)

Many poems evoke sensory images and sometimes have rhythm but do not rhyme. Children will enjoy all the different adjectives and actions, as in those applied to sand in the poem "The Beach":

> White sand,
>
> Sea sand,
>
> Warm sand,
>
> Kicking sand,
>
> Building sand,
>
> Watching sand
>
> As the waves roll in.

"I Have a Little Wagon" is an example of an action poem that has rhythm but does not rhyme:

> I have a little wagon, [*hold hand out, palm up*]
>
> It goes all around the town. [*move hand around*]
>
> I can pull it, [*pull hand in*]
>
> I can push it, [*push hand away*]
>
> I can turn it upside down. [*turn hand upside down*]

Word Play

Some poems, like "Willaby, Wallaby, Woo," play with words by juxtaposing interesting word patterns in a humorous and playful way:

> Willaby, wallaby, woo,
>
> An elephant stepped on you.
>
> Willaby, wallaby, wee,
>
> An elephant stepped on me.

In word play, we also include *tongue twisters* (poems that are challenging to recite because they play with words that are difficult to pronounce in succession). A well-known example is the poem "Fuzzy Wuzzy":

> Fuzzy Wuzzy was a bear.
>
> Fuzzy Wuzzy had no hair.
>
> Fuzzy Wuzzy wasn't fuzzy,
>
> Was he?

Humorous Verse

Humorous verse draws children's attention to absurdities as well as to the sounds and rhythms of language. Sometimes these humorous verses tell nonsense stories. A good example is the poem "There Once Was a Queen":

> There once was a queen
>
> Whose face was green.
>
> She ate her milk
>
> And drank her bread,
>
> And got up in the morning
>
> To go to bed.

Songs

Songs are musical texts originally intended to be sung. An example is the poem "Good Morning to You":

> Good morning to you!
>
> Good morning to you!
>
> We're all in our places
>
> With bright shining faces.
>
> Oh, this is the way to start a great day!

You may know the traditional tunes to the songs we have included in this volume. If you don't, compose your own or simply have children chant them while enjoying the rhythm and rhyme.

Action Songs and Poems

Action poems involve action along with rhythm and rhyme. An example is the poem "Pease Porridge Hot":

> Pease porridge hot, [*clap own hands*]
>
> Pease porridge cold, [*clap partner's hands*]
>
> Pease porridge in the pot, [*clap own hands*]
>
> Nine days old. [*clap partner's hands*]
>
>
> Some like it hot, [*one fist on top of the other*]
>
> Some like it cold, [*alternate fists, placing the other on top*]
>
> Some like it in the pot, [*clap partner's hands*]
>
> Nine days old. [*clap own hands*]

This category also includes *jump-rope songs*, traditional rhymes that children originally chanted while they jumped rope. An example is the poem "Teddy Bear, Teddy Bear":

> Teddy bear, teddy bear,
> Turn around.
>
> Teddy bear, teddy bear,
> Touch the ground.

Children can chant and act out jump-rope songs. There are also chants that accompany games or are simply enjoyable to say together. Chants, like songs, showcase rhythm and rhyme.

Concept Poems

Poems in this category focus on concepts such as numbers, days of the week, colors, ordinal words, seasons, and any other category of information. An example is the poem "Five Little Ducks Went in for a Swim":

> Five little ducks went in for a swim.
> The first little duck put his head in.
> The second little duck put his head back.
> The third little duck said, "Quack, quack, quack."
> The fourth little duck with his tiny brother
> Went for a walk with his father and mother.

This poem contains ordinal words (*first, second, third, fourth*) and the synonyms *little* and *tiny*.

These verses are not only engaging but also easy to learn. As children learn them, they will be repeating the vocabulary that surrounds important concepts.

In the category of concept poems, we also include name poems, which really transcend categories. Many verses present a wonderful opportunity to substitute children's names for names or words already there. In the poem "Pat-a-cake," you can substitute different children's names (and their first letters) for *Tommy*. Some of the names will not rhyme with *me*, but children will not mind. There are other rhymes included in this collection, with blank lines for children to fill in their names. "Come, Butter, Come," "Rain, Rain, Go Away," and "Who Is Wearing Red?" are some examples.

Many of the verses in the book also offer similar innovations, so look for opportunities. Children will love substituting their own words and phrases. They will develop ownership for the writing and, in the process, become more sensitive to rhymes, syllables, and word patterns.

Fifty Ways to Use Poems—Plus!

Below we suggest fifty specific ways to use the poems in this volume. Plus, you will notice that each poem includes an instructional suggestion: an easy way to refine and extend the learning and enjoyment potential of each poem. You will find many more ways to engage children in joyful play with oral and written language. The rich collection of poems in this volume can be reproduced, analyzed, or simply read aloud. Enjoy!

Decisions about using poetry depend on your purposes for instruction and the age of the children. By going over favorites again and again, children will internalize rhymes and develop awareness of new language structures. They will become more sensitive to the sounds of language and take pleasure in it. In kindergarten, focus more on attention to print, but be sure to enjoy the poem several times before working on the details. Try out suggestions of the following as appropriate to kindergarten:

1. **Marching to rhymes** Marching around the room while chanting a poem will help children feel the rhythm.

2. **Puppet show** Have children make stick, finger, or sock puppets of their favorite poetry characters and act out the poem as their friends read it. Alternatively, have the puppet say the poem.

3. **Storyboards** Have children draw or paint a backdrop that represents the scene from a rhyme or song. Then have them make cutout figures and glue them on popsicle sticks so that they can move the puppets around in front of the backdrop.

4. **Listening for rhymes** Have children clap or snap their fingers when they come to a rhyming word. They can also say the rhyming word softer (or louder) or mouth the word without making a sound.

5. **Responding** Divide the class in half. Taking a familiar poem, have half the group read (or say) the poem up to the rhyming word and then stop. Let the other half of the class shout the rhyming word.

6. **Recorded poems** Record specific poems on a device so that children can listen independently at a listening center. Include card stock copies of the poems, and show children how to follow along with the recordings.

7. **Class poetry recording** As children learn poems, gradually add to a class recording of their poetry reading or chanting. Keep a table of contents for the audio on a chart and/or place the taped poems in a book. Children can listen to the audio while following along in the book.

8. **Poem pictures** After reading a poem aloud at different times of the day, have children make pictures to go with it and display them with the poem. Duplicate individual copies of a simple poem and ask each child to illustrate it.

9. **Word endings** Write the poem in large print on a chart or on strips for a pocket chart. After many readings of a poem on a large chart, help children notice words that rhyme and specific vocabulary. They can use a masking card or highlighter tape to mark these words.

10. **Poem innovations** Engage children in noticing and using the language syntax in the poem to create their own similar versions. For example, insert different names in the poem "Jack, Be Nimble" or different foods in the poem "I Like Chocolate."

11. **Personal poetry books** Have children make their own personal poetry books by gluing the poems they experienced in shared reading into spiral notebooks and then illustrating them. Over time they will have a large personal collection of poems to take home.

12. **Little poem books** Make individual poem books, with one line of a poem on each page (for example, "One, two, buckle my shoe"). Children can illustrate each page, read the book, and take it home.

13. **Poem performances** Children can perform the poems after they learn them by sometimes adding sound effects with rhythm instruments such as sticks and drums or by clapping and snapping their fingers.

14. **Responsive reading** Find poems such as "Are You Sleeping?" that lend themselves to recitation by two or more speakers. Groups of children read questions and answers or alternate lines.

15. **Poetry play** Lead children in saying their favorite poems while they line up, as they walk through an area in which their talking will not disturb other classes, or any time they have a moment of wait time.

16. **Line-up poems** When passing out of the room for recess or lunch, play games in which children say or finish a line of a poem in order to take their place in line.

17. **Rhyming cloze** Read poems, asking children to join in only on the rhyming words. Put highlighter tape on the rhyming words.

18. **Finger poems and action poems** Make finger plays from poems. Act out poems with motions involving the entire body. We have included finger play and action directions for many poems, but you can make up many more.

19. **Poem posters** Use art materials (colored and/or textured paper, pens, crayons, paints) to illustrate poems on charts for the whole group to enjoy, or for children to enjoy individually in their personal poetry books.

20. **Poems with blanks** Give children individual copies of poems with a blank space in which they can write their names (or you can write it for them).

21. **Mystery words** In shared reading of a familiar poem, leave out key words but show the first letter so that children can check their reading. You can also use sticky notes and then uncover the word to check it.

22. **Poem displays** Display a poem in several places in the room; children find the poem and use chopstick pointers to read it in small and large versions.

23. **Poetry box** Make a poetry box that contains slightly enlarged and illustrated versions of familiar poems; children can take them out and read them to a classmate.

24. **Poetry board** Make a theme poetry board using poems that explore a concept (for example, animals or vegetables).

25. **Tongue twisters** Make up tongue twisters using the names of children in the class and have them illustrate the verses; for example, Carol carries cookies, carrots, candy, and cucumbers in a cart.

26. **Pocket chart** Place poems on sentence strips in a pocket chart for a variety of activities: substituting words to innovate on the text; highlighting words, letters, or parts of words with colored highlighter tape; putting sentence strips in order for reading; and masking words to make predictions.

27. **Poem puzzles** Have children cut a poem into strips, mix them up, order them, and glue them on paper in the correct order. Then have them use art materials to illustrate the text. Create a simple strip template to photocopy for many different poems.

28. **Class poem or song books** Take one simple, familiar poem and put each line on one page of an oversized class book. Staple the book together. Children can illustrate it and read it to others.

29. **Sequencing poems** Once they have internalized a poem, kindergarteners can write one line of a simple poem on separate pages, staple the pages together as a book, illustrate the pages, and then read their books to others.

30. **More songs and poems** Be on the alert for popular songs that children like or street rhymes that they know. Take appropriate verses from these songs and add them to the poetry collection.

31. **Poem plays** Create a play from the poem. Read the poem (children may join in) while several children act it out.

32. **Poetry dress-up** Collect some simple dress-up items related to the rhymes and poems in your collection. Invite the children to dress up for the poem reading.

33. **Poetry party** Have a party to which everyone comes dressed as a character from a poem (props may be made of paper). The group has to guess which poem is represented and then read the poem to the child representing that character.

34. **Character bulletin board** Each child draws a favorite character from a poem and then cuts the figure out. Use interactive writing to create labels for each character on the board.

35. **Poem mashup** Take two favorite poetry characters and have them "meet" each others' poems by including or switching their names.

36. **Favorite poetry recording** Prepare a poetry recording of the children's favorite poems, paper copies of which you can place in a box. Ask the principal, librarian, parents, and other teachers to contribute to the recordings. Children will enjoy listening to the different voices and following the words.

37. **Poetry picnic** Many poems have something to do with food. For example, "curds and whey" is similar to cottage cheese. After children have learned a lot of verses, make a list of foods. Consider bringing in samples of the food your class listed. Then children can read or say the poem while eating the food. Be sure to check with families for food allergies and get permission.

38. **Poetry pairs** Children find two poems that go together in some way. They bring the two poems to sharing time and tell how they are alike. You can make a class book of poem pairs with (illustrated) connected poems on opposite pages.

39. **Poetry landscape mural** Children paint a background on which they can glue different landscape mural poetry characters. This mural requires some planning.

For example, you would need to draw a mountain for the bear to go over in the poem "The Bear Went over the Mountain."

40. **Poetry sort** Have a box of poems on cards that children know very well and can read. They can read the poems and sort them in any way they want to: e.g., theme (happy, silly, sad), topic (mice, girls, boys, bears), and the way they rhyme (two lines, every other line, no rhyme).

41. **Poems in shapes** Have children read a poem and then glue the poem on a shape (give them a template) that represents it. For example, the poem "Window Watching" could be on or near a window.

42. **Mixed-up poem** Place a familiar poem on sentence strips in the pocket chart. Mix it up and have children help you rebuild it by saying the lines and looking for the next one. You can also have a correct model displayed beside the cut-up version so that they can check it. Soon children will be able to perform this action on their own.

43. **Picture words** Have children draw pictures for key words in a poem and display them right above the word on a chart.

44. **Hunting for words** Using flyswatters with rectangular holes in the center (or masking cards), have children hunt for particular words or words that rhyme with or start like another.

45. **Word location** Display a familiar poem in the pocket chart, but leave some blanks. Give children the missing key words. Stop when you come to the key word and ask who has it. Children will need to think about beginning sounds and letters when finding where they go.

46. **Word match** Place one line of a poem in the pocket chart and have children rebuild the line by matching individual words under the line.

47. **Builder poem** Give each child in a group one word from a poem, written in large print on a card. Have the rest of the class line up these children so that the word order is correct. Then have children take turns walking down the line and saying the poem by pointing to each child and his or her word. Alternatively, have children place the cards in a pocket chart one at a time. They will have to notice when their assigned words come next.

48. **Looking at high-frequency words** The words children encounter over and over in poems will form a core of words that they know and can recognize rapidly. You can have children locate the words to draw attention to them. They can also match word cards by placing like words on top of the words in the poem. An interesting exercise is to create high-frequency words in different fonts. Be sure the words are clear and recognizable. Matching these words to words on a chart or in the pocket chart creates an additional challenge in looking at the features of letters.

49. **Poetry newsletter** Send home a monthly newsletter that tells parents the poems children have learned and provides some poems they can sing or say at home.

50. **Class poetry book** Collect favorite poems into a class book that is small enough to be portable. Children take turns bringing the book home. They can read the poems to friends or family members.

Poetry Links to Phonics Lessons

In *Fountas & Pinnell Phonics, Spelling, and Word Study Lessons, Kindergarten* under Connect Learning Across Contexts, you will find Shared Reading recommendations that enable you to connect learning across the contexts shown in A Design for Responsive Literacy Teaching. Often, the shared reading recommendations suggest you turn to *Sing a Song of Poetry* for instructional follow-up using particular poems, songs, and verse. This list links many phonics lessons to a specific poem that extends and refines the instructional aim of the lesson; however, you will notice that not all lessons are linked to a poem, and sometimes, a lesson is linked to two or more poems. What does this mean? The links are completely flexible! Feel free to find and make your own links, and do not feel compelled to use every poem we recommend.

The primary goal of this collection is, quite literally, to sing a song of poetry! Invite children to chant, recite, echo, and play with the poems. Above all, *Sing a Song of Poetry* is meant to inspire a love of language.

Early Literacy Concepts

ELC 1 Bow-Wow-Wow; The Alphabet Song; Billy, Billy

ELC 2 Jack, Jack; Good Morning; Jack, Be Nimble

ELC 3 Someone's Birthday; Jerry Hall; Go to Bed

ELC 4 Charlie over the Ocean; Good Morning; Apples, Peaches

ELC 5 Jack, Jack; Sally, Go 'Round

ELC 6 Elizabeth, Elspeth, Betsey, and Bess; Jack and Jill

ELC 7 Fido; Jack and Jill; Little Bo-Peep

ELC 8 Gray Squirrel; Color Song; Roses Are Red

Phonological Awareness

PA 1 Dance a Merry Jig; A-hunting We Will Go

PA 2 Every Morning at Eight O'Clock; Jack, Jack

PA 3 High and Low; Pease Porridge Hot

PA 4 Red, White, and Blue; Six Little Ducks

PA 5 Stretching Fun; Stop, Look, and Listen

PA 6 Dormy, Dormy, Dormouse; Bouncing Ball

PA 7 I'm a Choo-Choo Train; Ladybug! Ladybug!; I'm Dusty Bill

PA 8 Puppies and Kittens; Little Jack Horner; Open, Shut Them

PA 9 Higglety, Pigglety, Pop!; Apple Harvest; Ring Around the Rosie

PA 10 I Measure Myself; Apples, Peaches; Five Fat Peas

Letter Knowledge

LK 18 Diddlety, Diddlety, Dumpty; Make a Pancake; Jumping Joan

LK 19 I Clap My Hands to Make a Sound; My Little Sister; See-Saw, Marjorie Daw

LK 20 How Many Days?; The Whole Duty of Children

LK 23 There Was an Old Woman Who Lived in a Shoe; Teeter-Totter; Mix a Pancake

Letter-Sound Relationships

LSR 1 Three Blind Mice; Snail, Snail

LSR 2 Willaby, Wallaby, Woo; Chickery, Chickery, Cranny, Crow

LSR 3 Dickory, Dickory, Dare!; This Is the Way We Wash Our Face

LSR 4 Diddlety, Diddlety, Dumpty; Two Little Black Birds

LSR 5 I Clap My Hands to Make a Sound; Teddy Bear, Teddy Bear

LSR 6 Five Fingers on Each Hand; Five Little Froggies

LSR 7 Here Is a House; Diddlety, Diddlety, Dumpty; Chickery, Chickery, Cranny, Crow

LSR 8 Five Fat Pumpkins; Pease, Porridge, Hot; Little White Rabbit

Spelling Patterns

SP 1 A Frog Sat on a Log; I Can Do It Myself; Five Fat Peas

SP 2 There Once Was an Old Woman; This Old Man; We Can; The Muffin Man

SP 3 My Head; Make a Pancake; The Cat

SP 4 Five Little Snowmen; Rain, Rain, Go Away; How Many Days?

SP 5 Hiccup, Hiccup; Pat-a-Cake; As I Was Walking

SP 6 Go to Bed Early; The Elephant Goes Like This; Pease Porridge Hot

SP 7 Go to Bed Early; Teeter Totter

High-Frequency Words

HFW 1 My Head; As I Was Going Along; To Market, to Market;

HFW 2 Puppies and Kittens; Fiddle-de-dee; Did You Ever See a Lassie?; Jack-in-the-box

HFW 3 Why Rabbits Jump; The Elephant Goes Like This; Puppies and Kittens

HFW 4 When Ducks Get Up in the Morning; Pease Porridge Hot; Little Jack Sprat

HFW 5 There Once Was a Queen; Who Stole the Cookies?; Twinkle, Twinkle, Little Star; Clap Your Hands

HFW 6 Here We Go; Hey Diddle Diddle; Baby Mice; Blow, Wind, Blow

HFW 7 Five Fingers on Each Hand; Little Red Apple; I Clap My Hands

Word Meaning/Vocabulary

WMV 1 Red, White, and Blue; Color Song

WMV 2 Gray Squirrel; Roses Are Red; Who Is Wearing Red?

WMV 3 One, Two, Three, Four; One Potato, Two Potato

WMV 4 Five Fat Pumpkins; Jumping Beans

WMV 5 How Many Days?; Tommy Snooks

WMV 6 How Many Days?; Today

WMV 7 Five Little Ducks Went in for a Swim; Five Little Monkeys on the Bed; My Little Sister

Word Structure

WS 1 What's the Weather?; Charlie over the Ocean

WS 2 I'm a Little Acorn Brown; There Was an Old Woman Who Lived in a Shoe; Skip to My Lou; Color Song; Fuzzy Wuzzy

WS 3 Five Fingers on Each Hand; Puppies and Kittens

WS 4 All by Myself; Hot Cross Buns; Here Are My Ears

Word-Solving Actions

WSA 1 Grandpa Grig; Little Jack Horner; Little Miss Muffet

WSA 2 Five Fingers on Each Hand; Bouncing Ball

WSA 3 Hiccup, Hiccup; Elsie Marley

WSA 4 Hiccup, Hiccup; Elsie Marley

WSA 5 The Mocking Bird; Who Stole the Cookies?; Little Red Apple

WSA 7 Rig-a-jig-jig; Chickery, Chickery, Cranny, Crow

WSA 8 Three Men in a Tub; Blackberries

WSA 9 Five Fat Pumpkins; Dance a Merry Jig

A-hunting We Will Go

Oh, a-hunting we will go,

A-hunting we will go,

We'll catch a fox and put him in a box,

And then we'll let him go.

SUGGESTION: After children learn this song, substitute other animal names and words that rhyme—the sillier the better: e.g., *whale–pail*; *skunk–trunk*; *snail–jail*; *bear–chair*.

fold here

All by Myself

These are things I can do

All by myself.

I can comb my hair and fasten my shoe

All by myself.

I can wash my hands and wash my face

All by myself.

I can put my toys and blocks in place

All by myself.

ACTIONS:

These are things I can do

All by myself. [point to self]

I can comb my hair and fasten my shoe [point to hair and shoe]

All by myself. [point to self]

I can wash my hands and wash my face [pretend to wash hands and face]

All by myself. [point to self]

I can put my toys and blocks in place [pretend to put things away]

All by myself. [point to self]

May be photocopied for classroom use. ©2018 by Irene C. Fountas and Gay Su Pinnell from *Sing a Song of Poetry, Kindergarten*. Portsmouth, NH: Heinemann.

fold here

SUGGESTION: There are lots of details to act out as the class learns this verse. Have children practice the poem with a partner or small group. Different groups can act out each specific action.

The Alphabet Song

A – B – C – D – E – F – G,

H – I – J – K – L – M – N – O – P,

Q – R – S,

T – U – V,

W – X,

Y and Z.

Now I've said my ABCs.

Tell me what you think of me.

May be photocopied for classroom use. ©2018 by Irene C. Fountas and Gay Su Pinnell from *Sing a Song of Poetry, Kindergarten.* Portsmouth, NH: Heinemann.

SUGGESTION: Almost all children know this song by the time they go to school. Encourage everyone to chime in with gusto.

fold here

Apple Harvest

Up in the green orchard,

There is a green tree,

The finest of pippins that ever you see.

The apples are ripe and ready to fall,

And Richard and Robin shall gather them all.

May be photocopied for classroom use. ©2018 by Irene C. Fountas and Gay Su Pinnell from *Sing a Song of Poetry, Kindergarten*. Portsmouth, NH: Heinemann.

SUGGESTION: Discuss the words *orchard* and *pippins*. Substitute children's names for *Richard* and *Robin*.

Apples, Peaches

Apples, peaches,

Pears, plums,

Tell me when your

Birthday comes.

SUGGESTION: Help children learn the months of the year by reciting this rhyme. Chant it repeatedly, following up with the name of each month of the year. Have children raise their hands or stand up if their birthday occurs in the month that is said.

fold here

Are You Sleeping?

Are you sleeping, are you sleeping,

Brother John? Brother John?

Morning bells are ringing,

Morning bells are ringing,

Ding, ding, dong,

Ding, ding, dong.

FRENCH TRANSLATION:

Frère Jacques, Frère Jacques,

Dormez-vous? Dormez-vous?

Sonnez les matines,

Sonnez les matines,

Din, din, don,

Din, din, don.

May be photocopied for classroom use. ©2018 by Irene C. Fountas and Gay Su Pinnell from *Sing a Song of Poetry, Kindergarten*. Portsmouth, NH: Heinemann.

fold here

SUGGESTION: Have children pretend to be asleep. Wake them up one at a time, speeding up the tempo as you say their names aloud. Let them create sound effects by ringing bells or tapping glasses containing different levels of water. Try this as a two- or three-part round by asking each successive group to begin singing when the previous group has finished line two. The class might also slenjoy learning the French version.

As I Was Going Along

As I was going along, along,

A-singing a comical song, song, song,

The lane that I went was so long, long, long,

And the song that I sang was so long, long, long,

And so I went singing along.

SUGGESTION: This is a good poem to sing or chant as children march around the room. Children may notice that every line has the same sounds at the end: *song, long, along*.

fold here

As I Was Walking

As I was walking near the lake,

I met a little rattlesnake.

He ate so much jelly-cake,

It made his little belly ache.

fold here

SUGGESTION: Have children rub their tummies at the end. You can change this poem by substituting colors or other adjectives like *yellow snake*, *slimy snake*, or *wiggly snake*.

Baa, Baa, Black Sheep

Baa, baa, black sheep,

Have you any wool?

Yes sir, yes sir, three bags full.

One for the master,

And one for the dame,

And one for the little boy

Who lives down the lane.

VARIATION:

Moo, moo, brown cow,
Have you any milk?
Yes miss, three jugs smooth as silk.
One for you,
And one for me,
And one for the little cat
Who sits in the tree.

SUGGESTION: Teach the class this rhyme. Then ask one group of children to say or sing the question and a second group to say or sing the response. Have children hold up one finger each time the word *one* is repeated. Help them come up with additional versions or variations of this rhyme, such as the one provided.

fold here

Baby Mice

Where are the baby mice?

Squeak, squeak, squeak.

I cannot see them.

Peek, peek, peek.

Here they come

From a hole in the wall,

One, two, three, four, five

In all!

SUGGESTION: Children enjoy pretending to be squeaking, peeking baby mice. (Masks, made from paper plates attached to tongue depressors, make it even more fun.) Have one half of the class be mice while the other half recites the poem. Then trade roles. Who is looking for these mice? A lost mouse, a child, a cat? There are many ways to interpret and share this nursery rhyme.

Baby Seeds

In a milkweed cradle, snug and warm,

Baby seeds are hiding safe from harm.

Open wide the cradle, hold it high,

Come along wind, help them fly.

May be photocopied for classroom use. ©2018 by Irene C. Fountas and Gay Su Pinnell from *Sing a Song of Poetry, Kindergarten*. Portsmouth, NH: Heinemann.

ACTIONS:

In a milkweed cradle, snug and warm, [*close fingers into fist*]

Baby seeds are hiding safe from harm.

Open wide the cradle, hold it high, [*open hand and hold it up high*]

Come along wind, help them fly. [*wiggle fingers*]

SUGGESTION: If no children are allergic, bring in milkweed so the class can see the *milkweed cradle*. Many other seeds—like dandelion seeds—fly on the wind. Look at some seeds together.

fold here

The Beach

White sand,

Sea sand,

Warm sand,

Kicking sand,

Building sand,

Watching sand

As the waves roll in.

May be photocopied for classroom use. ©2018 by Irene C. Fountas and Gay Su Pinnell from *Sing a Song of Poetry, Kindergarten.* Portsmouth, NH: Heinemann.

SUGGESTION: This poem evokes sensory images. Children might create other poems with descriptive words (*green grass*) or action words (*mowing grass*).

The Bear Went over the Mountain

The bear went over the mountain,

The bear went over the mountain,

The bear went over the mountain,

To see what he could see.

And all that he could see,

And all that he could see,

Was the other side of the mountain,

The other side of the mountain,

The other side of the mountain,

The other side of the mountain,

Was all that he could see.

May be photocopied for classroom use. ©2018 by Irene C. Fountas and Gay Su Pinnell from *Sing a Song of Poetry, Kindergarten*. Portsmouth, NH: Heinemann.

SUGGESTION: Have children sing this rhyme to the tune of "For He's a Jolly Good Fellow." It's lots of fun, especially while reading along with Rosemary Wells's picture book, *The Bear Went over the Mountain*. Children will enjoy making a simple mural and showing the bear (as a stick puppet) going over the mountain.

fold here

Bedtime

Down with the lambs,

Up with the lark,

Run to bed, children,

Before it gets dark.

SUGGESTION: Help children understand the references to going to bed early (*Down with the lambs*) and getting up early (*Up with the lark*). After they've learned the verse, have one group read the first line, a different group read the second line, and everyone read the last two lines.

Beets

I eat my beets with jelly;

I eat all afternoon.

It makes them really smelly,

But it keeps them on the spoon.

SUGGESTION: Children will enjoy inventing variations of this nonsense poem: e.g., *I eat my broccoli with jelly.* See another variation of this rhyme, "Peas," also in this volume.

fold here

Big and Small

I can make myself real big

By standing up straight and tall.

But when I'm tired of being big,

I can make myself get small.

fold here

SUGGESTION: Children can make themselves big, tall, and small as they recite this poem. They are learning different ways to move in space.

Big Turkey

There was a big turkey on a steep green hill,

And he said, "Gobble, gobble, gobble, gobble."

His tail spread out like a big feather fan,

And he said, "Gobble, gobble, gobble, gobble."

SUGGESTION: After children learn the poem, they can join together in a turkey rhythm band. Have them use tambourines, rhythm sticks, paper towel rolls, and spoons to accentuate the beat.

fold here

Billy, Billy

"Billy, Billy, come and play,

While the sun shines bright as day."

"Yes, my friend, that's what I'll do,

Because I like to play with you."

ADDITIONAL VERSES:

"Billy, Billy, have you seen

Sam and Betsy on the green?"

"Yes, my friend, I saw them pass,

Skipping over the nice cut grass."

"Billy, Billy, come along,

And I will sing a funny song.

fold here

SUGGESTION: Read this poem as question and answer. Substitute a child's name in the first line and have that child answer.

Bingo

There was a farmer who had a dog,

And Bingo was his name-o.

B – i – n – g – o,

B – i – n – g – o,

B – i – n – g – o,

And Bingo was his name-o.

VARIATION:

There was a cowboy rode a horse,

And Dusty was his name-o.

D – u – s – t – y,

D – u – s – t – y,

D – u – s – t – y,

And Dusty was his name-o.

SUGGESTION: Sing this song once in its entirety. The second time through, leave off the *B* and substitute a clap, a finger snap, or other short sound. The next time through, clap (or finger snap, etc.) for *B* and *I*. Continue until all five letters have been replaced with short sounds.

fold here

Blackberries

Blackberries, blackberries, on the hill.

How many pails can you fill?

Briers are thick and briers scratch,

But we'll pick all the berries

In the blackberry patch.

fold here

SUGGESTION: Have children snap their fingers or clap on the rhyming words. Also invite them to substitute other fruits for blackberries.

Blow, Wind, Blow

Blow, wind, blow! And go, mill, go!

That the miller can grind his corn,

That the baker can take it,

And into bread make it,

And bring us a loaf in the morn.

SUGGESTION: You many need to explain that a miller was a person who ground corn to make bread. Refer to Paul Galdone's retelling of the folktale *The Little Red Hen* found in the *Fountas & Pinnell Classroom™ Interactive Read-Aloud Collection, Kindergarten* (2018). When reading the poem, invite children to add simple sound effects for *blow* and *go*. Children will need support learning this archaic syntax.

fold here

Bouncing Ball

I'm bouncing, bouncing, everywhere,

I bounce and bounce into the air.

I'm bouncing, bouncing like a ball,

I bounce and bounce until I fall.

SUGGESTION: Bouncing is the ticket for enjoying these words. Invite children to bounce up and down as they say the rhyme before dropping to the floor.

Bow-Wow-Wow

Bow-wow-wow!

Whose dog art thou?

Little Tommy Tinker's dog,

Bow-wow-wow!

SUGGESTION: Have half the group play the dog and the other half play the questioner. Children will need help with the poem's archaic syntax (the words *art thou*) but will enjoy the fast repetition as well as reading a different child's name each time.

fold here

Cackle, Cackle, Mother Goose

Cackle, cackle, Mother Goose,

Have you any feathers loose?

Yes I have, my pretty fellow,

Just enough to fill a pillow.

May be photocopied for classroom use. ©2018 by Irene C. Fountas and Gay Su Pinnell from *Sing a Song of Poetry, Kindergarten*. Portsmouth, NH: Heinemann.

SUGGESTION: Children may be unfamiliar with the word *cackle* and may need to discuss the fact that many pillows are filled with feathers. Assign one child to read the final two lines. If children are looking at the print, they may notice all the double letters in five words.

The Cat

The cat sat asleep by the side of the fire.

The mistress snored loud as a pig.

Jack took up his fiddle by Jenny's desire,

And struck up a bit of a jig.

SUGGESTION: Three different children (cat, mistress, and Jack) can act out the poem while the rest say the rhyme. Children will enjoy adding a snoring sound to the end of the second line.

fold here

Catch Him, Crow

Catch him, crow! Carry him, kite!

Take him away until the apples are ripe.

When they are ripe and ready to fall,

Here comes baby, apples and all.

SUGGESTION: What's that baby doing up there, anyway? This poem can lead to an interesting discussion. Once they understand what is going on in this verse, children love to shout the line, *Catch him, crow! Carry him, kite!* This is a good poem for children to illustrate.

Charlie over the Ocean

Charlie over the ocean,

Charlie over the sea,

Charlie caught a blackbird,

But he can't catch me.

May be photocopied for classroom use. ©2018 by Irene C. Fountas and Gay Su Pinnell from *Sing a Song of Poetry, Kindergarten*. Portsmouth, NH: Heinemann.

SUGGESTION: Who is Charlie? What is going on here? Children will have lots of ideas. Substitute other children's names. Have children point to themselves at the end. Assign the first three lines to three smaller groups and have the whole group read the last line.

fold here

Chickery, Chickery, Cranny, Crow

Chickery, chickery, cranny, crow,

Went to the well to wash my toe.

When I got back, my chicken was gone.

What will I do from dusk to dawn?

May be photocopied for classroom use. ©2018 by Irene C. Fountas and Gay Su Pinnell from *Sing a Song of Poetry, Kindergarten.* Portsmouth, NH: Heinemann.

fold here

SUGGESTION: Ask children what they think is going on in this rhyme, and have them tell their own versions of the story. Invite children to clap on the rhyming words, whisper them, or say them loudly.

Chocolate Rhyme

One, two, three, cho—

One, two, three, co—

One, two, three, la—

One, two, three, te!

Stir, stir the chocolate.

May be photocopied for classroom use. ©2018 by Irene C. Fountas and Gay Su Pinnell from *Sing a Song of Poetry, Kindergarten*. Portsmouth, NH: Heinemann.

SUGGESTION: Have children count with their fingers and then mime stirring the chocolate. They can clap the word *chocolate* to identify syllable breaks or say the word slowly to identify sounds.

fold here

Clap Your Hands

Clap your hands, one, two, three.

Clap your hands just like me.

Wiggle your fingers, one, two, three.

Wiggle your fingers just like me.

fold here

SUGGESTION: Have the children clap their hands and wiggle their fingers as they say the rhyme. These movements strengthen children's hands and help them develop fine motor control, just as the words help them develop phonemic awareness and vocabulary. You can have children make up new motions as you go around in a circle (*Kick your foot, Rub your tummy,* and *Nod your head*).

Cobbler, Cobbler

Cobbler, cobbler, mend my shoe.

Get it done by half past two;

Stitch it up and stitch it down.

Then I'll give you half a crown.

fold here

SUGGESTION: Children are intrigued when they find out that a crown is an old-time coin, not just a special headdress worn by a king or queen. Pair this verse with the classic tale *The Elves and the Shoemaker* by the Brothers Grimm (2003).

Color Song

Red is the color for an apple to eat.

Red is the color for cherries, too.

Red is the color for strawberries.

I like red, don't you?

May be photocopied for classroom use. ©2018 by Irene C. Fountas and Gay Su Pinnell from *Sing a Song of Poetry, Kindergarten.* Portsmouth, NH: Heinemann.

ADDITIONAL VERSES:

Blue is the color for the big blue sky.

Blue is the color for baby things, too.

Blue is the color of my sister's eyes.

I like blue, don't you?

Yellow is the color for the great big sun.

Yellow is the color for lemonade, too.

Yellow is the color of a baby chick.

I like yellow, don't you?

Green is the color for the leaves on the trees.

Green is the color for green peas, too.

Green is the color of a watermelon.

I like green, don't you?

Orange is the color for oranges that grow.

Orange is the color for carrots, too.

Orange is the color of a pumpkin.

I like orange, don't you?

fold here

SUGGESTION: Using the same structure, create new verses for other colors, such as black, brown, gray, pink, and purple.

Come and Listen

Come and listen,

Come and listen,

To my song,

To my song.

Happy children singing,

Happy children singing,

Sing along,

Sing along.

SUGGESTION: This rhyme can be sung to the tune of "Are You Sleeping?" It's a good one to use as the class gathers for various activities.

fold here

Come, Butter, Come

Come, butter, come,

Come, butter, come.

_____'s at the garden gate,

Waiting with banana cake.

Come, butter, come.

SUGGESTION: Children probably won't know a lot about making butter. As they learn this poem, have them sit in a circle and pass around a tub of whipping cream. Have each child shake the container and hand it to the next person. The liquid will soon start to thicken. It won't be long before children notice that the liquid in the tub has stopped swishing around; it has become a solid. They have made butter! Spread the butter on crackers and eat them together. Be sure to first check for allergies or food sensitivities.

Cross Patch

Cross patch, draw the latch,

Sit by the fire and spin.

Take a cup and drink it up,

And let your neighbors in.

SUGGESTION: To the beat, have pairs of children perform the following sequence on the first two lines: clap thighs, clap hands, and clap partner's palms face front. Then on the last two lines, have pairs of children perform the following sequence: clap hands, clap thighs, clap hands, and clap partner's palms face front.

fold here

Cuckoo, Cuckoo

Cuckoo, cuckoo, cherry tree,

Cuckoo, cuckoo, cherry tree.

Catch a bird and give it to me.

Let the tree be high or low,

Sunshine, wind, or rain, or snow.

May be photocopied for classroom use. ©2018 by Irene C. Fountas and Gay Su Pinnell from *Sing a Song of Poetry, Kindergarten*. Portsmouth, NH: Heinemann.

SUGGESTION: Explain that a cuckoo is a kind of bird. Children will enjoy the contrast in this poem (*high* and *low*) as well as the weather words.

Dance a Merry Jig

This little pig danced a merry, merry jig.

This little pig ate candy.

This little pig wore a blue and yellow wig.

This little pig was a dandy.

But this little pig never grew very big,

And they called her itty bitty Mandy.

May be photocopied for classroom use. ©2018 by Irene C. Fountas and Gay Su Pinnell from *Sing a Song of Poetry, Kindergarten*. Portsmouth, NH: Heinemann.

fold here

SUGGESTION: Have children touch their fingers as they say the rhyme. Because there are so many specific details in this rhyme, it's great to use for directed drawing. See how many things children will include in their artwork as you read and reread the poem. In subsequent readings of the poem, substitute other names that rhyme with *Mandy*: e.g., *Andy*, *Sandy*, and *Randy*.

Dickory, Dickory, Dare!

Dickory, dickory, dare!

The pig flew up in the air;

The man in brown,

Soon brought him down.

Dickory, dickory, dare!

SUGGESTION: Introduce this variation after the more familiar verse "Hickory, Dickory, Dock!" along with the version "Hickory Dickory, Dore!" (both included in this book). Children will love to compare and perform the variations. Have three groups rehearse a variation and perform it for the other groups. Be sure to point out how the title and text change when substituting *d* for *h* in the word *hickory*. This is a good example to use when working with hearing and substituting sounds.

Did You Ever See a Lassie?

Did you ever see a lassie, a lassie, a lassie?

Did you ever see a lassie

Go this way and that?

Go this way and that way,

And this way and that way?

Did you ever see a lassie go this way and that?

fold here

SUGGESTION: Teach children the tune by singing or playing the song yourself or by playing a recording of it. Have groups of children sing this song as a question-and-answer exchange: *Did you ever . . . ? No, I never . . .* Substitute *laddie* for *lassie*. Expand the vocabulary by seeing what other things children may want to ask: *Did you ever see a space ship? Did you Yever see an elephant?* and so on. Write down children's responses and read them back together. Compile these responses in a class book.

Diddle, Diddle, Dumpling

Diddle, diddle, dumpling, my son John,

Went to bed with his breeches on.

One shoe off and one shoe on,

Diddle, diddle, dumpling, my son John.

fold here

SUGGESTION: Talk about the word *breeches* (meaning "trousers") and substitute other crazy things you could wear to bed. Children love coming up with ideas, from swimsuits to bike helmets. Substitute other children's names as well.

Diddlety, Diddlety, Dumpty

Diddlety, diddlety, dumpty,

The cat ran up the plum tree;

Half a crown to fetch her down,

Diddlety, diddlety, dumpty.

SUGGESTION: Point out that one meaning of *crown* is an old-time British coin. Children may want to substitute a *half-dollar*. They may notice that *diddlety* and *dumpty* have endings that sound alike. Have them say these words slowly and listen for the sounds.

fold here

A Diller, A Dollar

A diller, a dollar,

A ten o'clock scholar,

What makes you come so soon?

You used to come at ten o'clock,

But now you come at noon.

fold here

SUGGESTION: Children may not be familiar with the word *scholar*, so be sure to talk about the word's meaning Also, let children puzzle over whether noon is sooner or later than ten o'clock. Use a clock with movable hands or display it on a tablet to show the different times mentioned in the poem.

Doodlebug

Doodlebug, doodlebug, come get sweet milk.

Doodlebug, doodlebug, come get some butter.

Doodlebug, doodlebug, come get corn bread.

Doodlebug, doodlebug, come get supper.

SUGGESTION: Add instruments such as a xylophone or a tambourine to accompany *doodlebug* each time the word is read. Since the poem does not rhyme, it's easy to add lines to include children's favorite foods.

fold here

Dormy, Dormy, Dormouse

Dormy, dormy, dormouse,

Sleeps in his little house.

He won't wake up until suppertime,

And that won't be until half past nine.

fold here

SUGGESTION: Have children imagine a small animal that looks like a mouse and is very sleepy. Point out how *dormy* and *dormouse* start alike and how *house* and *mouse* rhyme.

Down by the Station

Down by the station,

Early in the morning,

See the little puffer-bellies,

All in a row.

See the engine driver,

Pull the little throttle.

Puff, puff! Toot, toot!

Off we go.

SUGGESTION: Simple instruments, such as a bell and a tambourine, can be used to emphasize the words *puff* and *toot*. Children will enjoy scooting around the room like a train. You can also have children sit in a line to read the poem, reaching and pulling their right arms for *Puff, puff!* and their left arms for *Toot, toot!*

fold here

Downy Duck

One day I saw a downy duck

With feathers on his back.

I said, "Good morning, downy duck."

And he said, "Quack, quack, quack."

SUGGESTION: A little duck puppet (with feathers on his back) is perfect for children to use to act out this poem. If you can't find a duck puppet, have children draw pictures of a duck, cut them out, and attach them to their index fingers using strips of construction paper glued to form a cylinder. Assign a child to read each of the dialogue parts.

The Elephant Goes Like This

The elephant goes like this, like that.

He's terribly big,

And he's terribly fat.

He has no fingers,

He has no toes,

But goodness gracious,

What a nose!

ACTIONS:

The elephant goes like this, like that. [*slowly move on all fours like an elephant*]

He's terribly big, [*stand up and reach arms high*]

And he's terribly fat. [*stretch arms out to the sides*]

He has no fingers, [*make a fist and hide fingers*]

He has no toes, [*wiggle toes*]

But goodness gracious,

What a nose! [*point to nose*]

SUGGESTION: Have a whole line of children troop through the classroom like elephants, swinging their trunks and swaying their bodies. Recite the poem together slowly, suggesting the rhythm of an elephant, while adding the motions.

fold here

Elizabeth, Elspeth, Betsey, and Bess

Elizabeth, Elspeth, Betsey, and Bess,

They all went together to seek a hen's nest;

They found a hen's nest with five eggs in,

They all took an egg, and left one in.

SUGGESTION: Substitute the names of four children in the class. Cut out representations of the characters, a hen's nest, and five eggs before affixing them to small magnets. Then have children retell the story as they manipulate the cutouts on a magnetic cookie sheet or whiteboard.

Elsie Marley

Elsie Marley's grown so fine,

She won't get up to feed the swine,

But lies in bed until eight or nine!

Lazy Elsie Marley.

SUGGESTION: Substitute children's names or nonsense two-part names for *Elsie Marley*. Children may not know that *swine* is another name for *pig* or that sleeping until eight or nine o'clock means sleeping past the start of school.

fold here

Every Morning at Eight O'Clock

Every morning at eight o'clock,

You can hear the mail carrier's knock.

Up jumps Katy to open the door,

One letter, two letters, three letters, four.

SUGGESTION: This poem is ideal for children to act out. You can prepare letter cards that spell children's names or list high-frequency words. These cards will serve as the letters that children pretend to receive in the mail. The child named in the poem can deliver the letters. You can substitute the name *Katy* with other names of children in the class.

The Farmer in the Dell

The farmer in the dell,

The farmer in the dell,

Hi-ho, the derry-o,

The farmer in the dell.

ADDITIONAL VERSES:

The farmer takes a wife.

The wife takes a child.

The child takes a nurse.

The nurse takes a cow.

The cow takes a dog.

The dog takes a cat.

The cat takes a rat.

The rat takes the cheese.

The cheese stands alone.

May be photocopied for classroom use. ©2018 by Irene C. Fountas and Gay Su Pinnell from *Sing a Song of Poetry, Kindergarten.* Portsmouth, NH: Heinemann.

SUGGESTION: Have children join hands and form a circle around one child chosen as the farmer. As they sing, have children walk in one direction around the farmer. At the end of each verse, the farmer chooses a classmate to join him or her in the middle. Continuing until everyone has been chosen may require repeating the song as the child representing cheese stands alone and then becomes the new farmer.

fold here

Father, Mother, and Uncle John

Father, Mother, and Uncle John

Went to market one by one.

Father fell off,

Mother fell off,

But Uncle John rode on and on.

And on,

And on,

And on,

And on,

And on . . .

SUGGESTION: Substitute children's names for *Uncle John*. What things might these characters ride to get to the market? Cars, dragons, horses, donkeys? Capture their ideas in a list on a chart or whiteboard. Read the ideas back as a group. Which kinds of rides do children think are logical?

Fiddle-de-dee

Fiddle-de-dee, fiddle-de-dee,

The fly shall marry the bumblebee.

They went to the hall, and married was she,

The fly has married the bumblebee.

fold here

SUGGESTION: Children will need practice to master the unusual syntax of this poem, but it will increase their awareness of the structure of written language. If children are looking at the poem, point out the double *ee* in words.

Fido

I have a little dog

And his name is Fido.

He is nothing but a pup.

He can stand on his hind legs

If you hold his front legs up.

SUGGESTION: Substitute the name *Fido* with the names of the children in your class (or other names the children may suggest). Ask children to draw dog pictures. Then ask them to place their dog drawings around the printed poem on a poetry chart. Ask children to say *up* and *pup* and to listen for the ending sound.

Five Fat Pumpkins

Five fat pumpkins sitting on a gate.

First one said, "Oh my, it's getting late."

Second one said, "There's a bat in the air."

Third one said, "We don't care."

Fourth one said, "Let's run, run, run."

Fifth one said, "Let's have some fun."

But *whooo* went the wind and out went the light

And five fat pumpkins rolled out of sight.

May be photocopied for classroom use. ©2018 by Irene C. Fountas and Gay Su Pinnell from *Sing a Song of Poetry, Kindergarten*. Portsmouth, NH: Heinemann.

SUGGESTION: This rhyme can be done as a finger play. While reciting the poem aloud, have children hold up five fingers and wiggle one for each pumpkin. Then have children cup their mouths and blow for the wind before rolling one hand over the other during the last line. Or, five children can sit as pumpkins on a gate and mime the actions of the poem as the rest of the class recites the words. Secretly tell one child to turn off the classroom lights on the words *out went the light*. Children also love making pumpkin puppets from cut paper and craft sticks.

fold here

Five Fingers on Each Hand

I have five fingers on each hand,

Ten toes on my two feet,

Two ears, two eyes,

One nose, one mouth,

With which to sweetly speak.

My hands can clap, my feet can tap,

My eyes can clearly see.

My ears can hear, my nose can sniff,

My mouth can say, "I'm me."

SUGGESTION: Have children indicate the appropriate body parts. You can use Lois Ehlert's picture book, *Hands*, with this rhyme as well. Have children trace their hands on construction paper and cut them out.

Five Little Ducks

Five little ducks went out one day,

Over the hills and far away,

Mother Duck said, "Quack, quack, quack, quack,"

But only four little ducks came back.

May be photocopied for classroom use. ©2018 by Irene C. Fountas and Gay Su Pinnell from *Sing a Song of Poetry, Kindergarten.* Portsmouth, NH: Heinemann.

SUGGESTION: After children have learned this verse and are familiar with the words, you can use it as a countdown poem. Eventually, the poem will count down to the last line, *But only one little duck came back.* Revisit this when you are working with number words. The last line changes during the *one little duck* verse: *And all the five little ducks came back.*

fold here

Five Little Ducks Went in for a Swim

Five little ducks went in for a swim.

The first little duck put his head in.

The second little duck put his head back.

The third little duck said, "Quack, quack, quack."

The fourth little duck with his tiny brother

Went for a walk with his father and mother.

May be photocopied for classroom use. ©2018 by Irene C. Fountas and Gay Su Pinnell from *Sing a Song of Poetry, Kindergarten.* Portsmouth, NH: Heinemann.

ACTIONS:

Five little ducks went in for a swim. [*wiggle fingers*]

The first little duck put his head in. [*put head forward*]

The second little duck put his head back. [*put head back*]

The third little duck said, "Quack, quack, quack." [*clap three times*]

The fourth little duck with his tiny brother

Went for a walk with his father and mother. [*walk fingers*]

fold here

SUGGESTION: Invite children to perform a little duck finger play while reciting the poem together.

Five Little Fingers

One little finger standing on its own.

Two little fingers, now they're not alone.

Three little fingers happy as can be.

Four little fingers go walking down the street.

Five little fingers, this one is a thumb.

Wave bye-bye because now we are done.

ACTIONS:

One little finger standing on its own. [*hold up index finger*]

Two little fingers, now they're not alone. [*add middle finger*]

Three little fingers happy as can be. [*add ring finger*]

Four little fingers go walking down the street. [*add little finger and wiggle all four fingers*]

Five little fingers, this one is a thumb. [*add thumb*]

Wave bye-bye because now we are done. [*wave goodbye*]

SUGGESTION: Teach the children the finger actions to go along with the rhyme. As a follow-up, share Lois Ehlert's picture book, *Hands*, which has a cardboard cover shaped like a work glove. The book shows all kinds of things hands can do.

fold here

Five Little Froggies

Five little froggies sitting on a well,

One looked up and down she fell.

Froggies jumped high,

Froggies jumped low,

Four little froggies dancing to and fro.

May be photocopied for classroom use. ©2018 by Irene C. Fountas and Gay Su Pinnell from *Sing a Song of Poetry, Kindergarten.* Portsmouth, NH: Heinemann.

SUGGESTION: Children will clamber to be froggies, jumping high and low and dancing to and fro as they act out the poem. The rest of the group can recite the poem. Once children are familiar with the verse, have them count down from *four little froggies* to *three little froggies* and so on. Try recreating the poem on a felt board or magnet board. Then ask the children to remove a frog with each verse they countdown.

Five Little Monkeys in a Tree

Five little monkeys

Swinging in a tree,

Teasing Mr. Crocodile,

"You can't catch me!"

Along comes Mr. Crocodile,

Quiet as can be.

Snap!

Four little monkeys

Swinging in a tree.

SUGGESTION: Children love to act out this rhyme. The most popular character is the crocodile who gets to *snap*. Have children continue the rhyme by substituting the appropriate numbers until all the monkeys have been snapped up by the crocodile.

fold here

Five Little Monkeys on the Bed

Five little monkeys jumping on the bed,

One fell off and bumped his head.

Mama called the doctor, and the doctor said,

"No more monkeys jumping on the bed!"

fold here

SUGGESTION: Children enjoy acting out this poem. You need five monkeys, the doctor, and Mama. Divvy up the roles among seven children. Ask the rest of the class to help by reading along. Continue the countdown by having one monkey leave the circle each time a monkey falls off the bed. Substitute another animal for variation.

Five Little Sausages

Five little sausages frying in a pan,

Sizzle, sizzle, sizzle, and one went BAM!

Four little sausages frying in a pan,

Sizzle, sizzle, sizzle, and one went BAM!

Three little sausages frying in a pan,

Sizzle, sizzle, sizzle, and one went BAM!

Two little sausages frying in a pan,

Sizzle, sizzle, sizzle, and one went BAM!

One little sausage frying in a pan,

Sizzle, sizzle, sizzle, and it went BAM!

SUGGESTION: Children enjoy shouting *BAM!* at the end of each verse and may clap spontaneously when they do so. You can also ask them to emphasize the /s/ and /z/ sounds of *sizzle* to suggest how these sausages sound when they cook. Have them hold up and wiggle five fingers on the first verse and then one fewer on each successive verse.

fold here

Five Little Snowmen

Five little snowmen happy and gay,

The first one said, "What a nice day!"

The second one said, "We'll cry no tears."

The third one said, "We'll stay for years."

The fourth one said, "But what happens in May?"

The fifth one said, "Look, we're melting away!"

SUGGESTION: As children learn the rhyme, have them hold up one hand and wiggle a different digit with each line. At the end, they can hold out a closed fist to indicate that all the snowmen are gone. Once they have learned the words, assign five children to read the quoted lines while the rest serve as narrators, reciting (in unison) the first line and the beginning of each successive line.

A Frog Sat on a Log

A frog sat on a log,

A-weeping for his daughter.

His eyes were red,

His tears he shed,

And he fell right into the water.

May be photocopied for classroom use. ©2018 by Irene C. Fountas and Gay Su Pinnell from *Sing a Song of Poetry, Kindergarten*. Portsmouth, NH: Heinemann.

SUGGESTION: Invite children to imagine what happened to Frog's daughter and why he is crying. Have them identify words in the rhyme that have the same ending sound.

fold here

Frosty Weather

Frosty weather,

Snowy weather,

When the wind blows,

We all go together.

fold here

SUGGESTION: Invite children to imagine the sound of the wind. Ask some to make wind sounds as the other children say the verse. They can also generate other words that go with *frosty* and *snowy*: e.g., *windy* and *chilly*.

Fuzzy Wuzzy

Fuzzy Wuzzy was a bear.

Fuzzy Wuzzy had no hair.

Fuzzy Wuzzy wasn't fuzzy,

Was he?

SUGGESTION: After children learn the poem and can say the words, have them discuss what Fuzzy Wuzzy looks like. Help them notice the subtle pronunciation difference between *wuzzy* and *was he* as well as the rising tone signaled by the question mark.

fold here

Georgy Porgy

Georgy Porgy, pudding and pie,

Kissed the girls and made them cry.

When the boys came out to play,

Georgy Porgy ran away.

May be photocopied for classroom use. ©2018 by Irene C. Fountas and Gay Su Pinnell from *Sing a Song of Poetry, Kindergarten.* Portsmouth, NH: Heinemann.

fold here

SUGGESTION: Have children clap twice on *Georgy* and twice on *Porgy* as they read or recite the rhyme.

Giddyup

Giddyup, giddyup,

One, two, three.

Giddyup, giddyup,

Come see me.

SUGGESTION: Have children take turns reading specific lines. Extend the rhyme by writing it on chart paper (or a pocket chart). Insert *four*, *five*, *six* and ask children if they can think of a rhyming line. Children easily figure out what actions go with *giddyup* and enjoy pretending to ride.

fold here

Go in and out the Window

Go in and out the window,

Go in and out the window,

Go in and out the window,

As we have done before.

fold here

SUGGESTION: This is a game song. Have children form a circle and raise clasped hands. The child who is "it" chooses a partner and grabs on at the waist. They go in and out the "windows" formed by classmates' raised arms. Then the chosen partner chooses another partner as the poem is repeated.

Go to Bed

Go to bed late,

Stay very small.

Go to bed early,

Grow very tall.

May be photocopied for classroom use. ©2018 by Irene C. Fountas and Gay Su Pinnell from *Sing a Song of Poetry, Kindergarten*. Portsmouth, NH: Heinemann.

SUGGESTION: Many rhymes recommend beneficial behavior. Discuss the importance of getting enough sleep. Ask children what helps them go to sleep at night. Teddy bears? Special blankets? Being told a bedtime story or sung a lullaby? Saying a poem or retelling a story in their head? Have children recite the rhyme together, crouching on the word *small* and stretching up high when they say *tall*.

fold here

Go to Bed Early

Go to bed early—wake up with joy,

Go to bed late—tired girl or boy;

Go to bed early—ready for play,

Go to bed late—moping all day;

Go to bed early—no pains or ills,

Go to bed late—doctors and pills;

Go to bed early—grow very tall,

Go to bed late—stay very small.

fold here

SUGGESTION: This is an old instruction rhyme showing the importance of a good night's sleep. After children are familiar with the words, have them create their own actions to accompany each line. How well can they improvise? Alternatively, try having two groups alternate reading the lines.

Gobble, Gobble, Gobble

Gobble, gobble, gobble,

Quack, quack, quack,

A turkey says gobble,

And a duck says quack.

SUGGESTION: Have different children take turns gobbling and quacking while reading this verse. Help them create new verses, ask them to suggest other animals and the sounds they make, and then arrange the words into this same pattern. Ask them to clap the syllables of the animal sounds in each line to see if their suggestions will match. *Meow, meow, meow; bow-wow-wow; oink, oink, oink;* and *moo, moo, moo* are some animal noises that can be substituted.

fold here

Good Morning

Good morning,

Good morning,

How are you?

How are you?

Very well, I thank you,

Very well, I thank you,

How about you?

How about you?

ADDITIONAL VERSES:

Good afternoon,

Good afternoon,

How are you?

How are you?

Very well, I thank you,

Very well, I thank you,

How about you?

How about you?

Good evening,

Good evening,

How are you?

How are you?

Very well, I thank you,

Very well, I thank you,

How about you?

How about you?

May be photocopied for classroom use. ©2018 by Irene C. Fountas and Gay Su Pinnell from *Sing a Song of Poetry, Kindergarten*. Portsmouth, NH: Heinemann.

fold here

SUGGESTION: This piggyback song can be sung to the tune of "Are You Sleeping?" Introduce the poem in the morning using the first verse and revisit with the other verses at appropriate times of the day. Children may create more wild and imaginative words to the tune.

Good Morning to You

Good morning to you!

Good morning to you!

We're all in our places

With bright shining faces.

Oh, this is the way to start a great day!

ADDITIONAL VERSES:

Good noontime to you!

Good noontime to you!

We're all feeling yummy

With food in our tummy.

Oh, this is the way to have a great day!

A goodbye to you!

A goodbye to you!

We'll leave as the day ends

and go home to see friends.

Oh, this is the way to end a great day!

SUGGESTION: This old song has some new verses, and children may want to create more. Teach it one verse at a time at the appropriate time of day. The song will become a good gathering verse when children arrive in the morning, return from lunch, and line up to leave.

fold here

Grandpa Grig

Grandpa Grig

Had a pig

In a field of clover;

Piggy died,

Grandpa cried,

And all the fun was over.

fold here

SUGGESTION: Create new verses with different names for Grandpa that rhyme with other animal names, such as *Grandpa Bog / Had a dog*.

Gray Squirrel

Gray squirrel, gray squirrel,

Swish your bushy tail.

Wrinkle up your funny nose,

Hold an acorn in your toes.

Gray squirrel, gray squirrel,

Swish your bushy tail.

ACTIONS:

Gray squirrel, gray squirrel, [*stand with hands on bent knees*]

Swish your bushy tail. [*wiggle the behind*]

Wrinkle up your funny nose, [*wrinkle nose*]

Hold an acorn in your toes. [*pinch index finger and thumb together*]

Gray squirrel, gray squirrel, [*stand with hands on bent knees*]

Swish your bushy tail. [*wiggle the behind*]

May be photocopied for classroom use. ©2018 by Irene C. Fountas and Gay Su Pinnell from *Sing a Song of Poetry, Kindergarten.* Portsmouth, NH: Heinemann.

SUGGESTION: Children enjoy performing the actions that accompany this rhyme. They also enjoy making hand puppets by drawing gray squirrels, cutting them out, and attaching them to craft sticks.

fold here

Great A

Great A, little a, bouncing B.

The cat's in the cupboard

And can't see me.

May be photocopied for classroom use. ©2018 by Irene C. Fountas and Gay Su Pinnell from *Sing a Song of Poetry, Kindergarten.* Portsmouth, NH: Heinemann.

SUGGESTION: Try replacing the letters *A*, *a*, and *B* with other uppercase and lowercase letters. You can change *great* to *big* or use the words *uppercase* and *lowercase*. Children can hold up large letter cards depicting the letters read aloud at appropriate points in the poem.

Head, Shoulders, Knees, and Toes

Head, shoulders, knees, and toes,

Knees and toes.

Head, shoulders, knees, and toes,

Knees and toes.

And eyes and ears and mouth and nose.

Head, shoulders, knees, and toes,

Knees and toes.

SUGGESTION: Sing the song in its entirety, having children touch their heads, their shoulders, their knees, their toes, their eyes, their ears, their mouths, and their noses. The second time through, omit the word *head* but still perform the motion. Then omit *shoulders, knees, toes, eyes, ears, mouth,* and *nose* one at time, still performing the motions while going faster and faster.

fold here

Hear the Lively Song

Hear the lively song

Of the frogs in yonder pond.

Crick, crick, crickety-crick,

Burr-ump!

fold here

SUGGESTION: After children know this verse, it's fun to orchestrate the whole poem between four groups: frogs in the pond, narrators, a group assigned solely to saying *crick, crick, crickety-crick* while snapping their fingers, and a group solely providing the sound *Burr-ump!*

Here Are My Ears

Here are my ears.

Here is my nose.

Here are my fingers.

Here are my toes.

Here are my eyes

Both open wide.

Here is my mouth

With white teeth inside.

Here is my tongue

That helps me speak.

Here is my chin

And here are my cheeks.

Here are my hands

That help me play.

Here are my feet

For walking today.

May be photocopied for classroom use. ©2018 by Irene C. Fountas and Gay Su Pinnell from *Sing a Song of Poetry, Kindergarten.* Portsmouth, NH: Heinemann.

SUGGESTION: Have children point to or display each body part as they go through all the verses. English language learners especially benefit from identifying body parts as they say the specific vocabulary. As an extension, have children draw a self-portrait and label the various parts of the body. You may want to work through the poem on chart paper and highlight or underline each body part so that children have a model for writing the words.

Here Are My Eyes

Here are my eyes,

One and two.

I can wink.

So can you.

When my eyes are open,

I see the light.

When they are closed,

It's dark as night.

ACTIONS:

Here are my eyes, [*point to both eyes using two fingers*]
One and two. [*point to one eye at a time*]
I can wink. [*wink while pointing to self*]
So can you. [*wink while pointing to others*]

When my eyes are open, [*open eyes wide*]
I see the light.
When they are closed, [*close eyes*]
It's dark as night.

fold here

SUGGESTION: The simple actions paired with this poem give children an exercise for their eyes. This is a good poem for children to recite with partners after they are familiar with the words. They face each other and take turns saying the first verse (emphasizing *me* and *you*); then, in unison, they recite the second verse.

Here Is a Bunny

Here is a bunny with ears so funny,

And here is his hole in the ground.

When a noise he hears, he pricks up his ears,

And hops into his hole so round.

May be photocopied for classroom use. ©2018 by Irene C. Fountas and Gay Su Pinnell from *Sing a Song of Poetry, Kindergarten*. Portsmouth, NH: Heinemann.

ACTIONS:

Here is a bunny with ears so funny, [*curl fingers over thumb and bounce two fingers to make bunny ears*]

And here is his hole in the ground. [*make hole with thumb and forefinger of other hand*]

When a noise he hears, he pricks up his ears, [*hold ears up straight*]

And hops into his hole so round. [*hop bunny over into the hole*]

SUGGESTION: Children love performing this finger play. Make sure they know the words before they focus on the hand movements. To add interest, freeze and unfreeze the action from time to time with a tap from your magic wand (a pencil with a star attached).

fold here

Here Is a House

Here is a house built up high,

With two tall chimneys reaching the sky.

Here are the windows.

Here is the door.

If we peep inside

We'll see a mouse on the floor.

May be photocopied for classroom use. ©2018 by Irene C. Fountas and Gay Su Pinnell from *Sing a Song of Poetry, Kindergarten.* Portsmouth, NH: Heinemann.

ACTIONS:

Here is a house built up high, [*stretch arms up, touching fingertips together like a roof*]

With two tall chimneys reaching the sky. [*stretch arms up separately*]

Here are the windows. [*make a square shape with hands*]

Here is the door. [*pantomime knocking*]

If we peep inside [*tilt head as if looking around a corner*]

We'll see a mouse on the floor. [*move fingers like a running mouse*]

SUGGESTION: Have children act out the rhyme. As an alternative, create a simple drawing of a big house with appropriate features and a cut-out door that opens, showing a cut-out mouse on a craft stick. Children can point to parts of the house, opening the door at the end.

Here Is the Sea

Here is the sea,

The wavy sea,

Here is a boat,

And here is me.

And all the fishes

Down below

Wiggle their tails

And away they go.

May be photocopied for classroom use. ©2018 by Irene C. Fountas and Gay Su Pinnell from *Sing a Song of Poetry, Kindergarten*. Portsmouth, NH: Heinemann.

ACTIONS:

Here is the sea, [*wave hands from side to side*]

The wavy sea, [*wiggle fingers*]

Here is a boat, [*cup hands like a boat*]

And here is me. [*point to yourself*]

And all the fishes [*wiggle fingers*]

Down below [*point down*]

Wiggle their tails [*wiggle fingers*]

And away they go. [*wiggle fingers behind back*]

fold here

SUGGESTION: Children love making motions for each line of this verse to indicate *the wavy sea, the boat, me,* and especially the *fishes* who *wiggle their tails* to swim away. Children may enjoy working with a partner.

Here We Go

Here we go—up, up, up.

Here we go—down, down, down.

Here we go—moving forward.

Here we go—moving backward.

Here we go—round and round and round.

May be photocopied for classroom use. ©2018 by Irene C. Fountas and Gay Su Pinnell from *Sing a Song of Poetry, Kindergarten*. Portsmouth, NH: Heinemann.

ACTIONS:

Here we go—up, up, up. [*stand up on toes*]

Here we go—down, down, down. [*crouch down low*]

Here we go—moving forward. [*take a step forward*]

Here we go—moving backward. [*take a step backward*]

Here we go—round and round and round. [*spin*]

fold here

SUGGESTION: Children need frequent opportunities to move around as they vocalize. They will enjoy this stretch-and-transition rhyme. The natural movements suggested for each line get children active while helping them remember the sequence of the words. Talk with children about words in the poem that are opposites; the actions will help them understand this concept.

Hey Diddle Diddle

Hey diddle diddle,

The cat and the fiddle,

The cow jumped over the moon;

The little dog laughed

To see such sport,

And the dish ran away with the spoon.

SUGGESTION: This rhyme is an all-time favorite and a great one to act out with stick puppets. Divide the group in half and have each group read three lines. Or have the whole class read lines 1 and 2 and assign specific children to read lines 3, 4, 5, and 6. Children will enjoy illustrating the poem as a mural or a four-page book (page 1 illustrates lines 1 and 2; page 2 illustrates line 3; page 3 illustrates lines 4 and 5; and page 4 illustrates line 6).

fold here

Hiccup, Hiccup

Hiccup, hiccup, go away!

Come again another day.

Hiccup, hiccup, when I bake,

I will give you a butter-cake.

fold here

SUGGESTION: After children have learned this poem, assign roles. Have one child say the words *hiccup, hiccup* (or pretend to hiccup and make the sound) while one group of children says the rest of the words and another group marks the beat with rhythm instruments. They can also substitute words for *butter*.

Hickory, Dickory, Dock!

Hickory, dickory, dock!

The mouse ran up the clock;

The clock struck one,

The mouse did run.

Hickory, dickory, dock!

SUGGESTION: This poem lends itself to accompanying actions: the motion of the pendulum (*hickory, dickory, dock*), the mouse running up or down the clock (fingers running up or down an arm), holding up one finger as the clock strikes one, and then the final back-and-forth pendulum motion. Variations of this poem appear in this book, including, "Hickory, Dickory, Dore!," "Higglety, Pigglety, Pop!," or "Dickory, Dickory, Dare!"

fold here

Hickory, Dickory, Dore!

Hickory, dickory, dore!

The dog sat on the floor;

The clock struck six,

The dog chewed sticks.

Hickory, dickory, dore!

May be photocopied for classroom use. ©2018 by Irene C. Fountas and Gay Su Pinnell from *Sing a Song of Poetry, Kindergarten*. Portsmouth, NH: Heinemann.

fold here

SUGGESTION: Children will enjoy comparing this variation to the previous poem, "Hickory, Dickory, Dock!," and other aforementioned variations. Groups of children can prepare a variation for presentation to the rest of the class.

Higglety, Pigglety, Pop!

Higglety, pigglety, pop!

The dog has eaten the mop;

The pig's in a hurry,

The cat's in a flurry.

Higglety, pigglety, pop!

SUGGESTION: Children will enjoy making mental pictures of the messy activity described. Invite them to add simple sounds using instruments like rhythm sticks, bells, or a tambourine to highlight the words *higglety*, *pigglety*, and *pop*. Help children to create new versions: e.g., *Higglety, pigglety, peen! / The dog has eaten the screen.*

fold here

High and Low

I reach my hands way up high,

I can almost touch the sky.

Then I bend way down low,

And touch the floor just so.

SUGGESTION: This verse has the side benefit of some accompanying exercise, so it's a good transition activity. As you teach the poem, add the movements called for by each line: reach hands high, stand on tiptoes, bend low, and touch the floor.

Hippity-Hop to the Candy Shop

Hippity-hop to the candy shop

To buy a stick of candy.

One for you and one for me

And one for sister Mandy.

fold here

SUGGESTION: The strong rhythm in this rhyme makes everyone want to hippity-hop and act out the poem. Have children say and clap the rhyming words (*candy, Mandy*) and think of others (*Andy, Sandy, dandy*).

Hokey Pokey

You put your right hand in,

You put your right hand out,

You put your right hand in,

And you shake it all about.

You do the Hokey Pokey

And you turn yourself around,

That's what it's all about.

fold here

SUGGESTION: This is a lively break from the day's routine. It adds to the fun to play a recorded version of the song, if you have it, as children form a circle, put their left hand (or other specified body part) into and out of the circle, and then shake it. On the line, *You do the Hokey Pokey*, have them raise both arms and wiggle their fingers as they turn around.

Hot Cross Buns

Hot cross buns! Hot cross buns!

One-a-penny, two-a-penny,

Hot cross buns!

If you have no daughters,

Give them to your sons,

One-a-penny, two-a-penny,

Hot cross buns!

SUGGESTION: Explain that hot cross buns are bread rolls with white icing that criss-crosses on them. Children will enjoy clapping three times every time they read aloud, *Hot cross buns*!

fold here

How Many Days?

How many days do we have to play?

Saturday, Sunday, Monday—

Tuesday, Wednesday, Thursday,

Friday, Saturday, Sunday.

May be photocopied for classroom use. ©2018 by Irene C. Fountas and Gay Su Pinnell from *Sing a Song of Poetry, Kindergarten*. Portsmouth, NH: Heinemann.

fold here

126

SUGGESTION: This poem helps children learn the days of the week. Create a slightly different verse by repeating the words of line 1 and then beginning line 2 with a different day. Since days of the week are always in the same order, starting with a new day changes the whole poem. Have children take turns picking a new day with which to begin. They can clap as they say each day. If children are looking at the poem, they can count the days.

Humpty Dumpty

Humpty Dumpty sat on a wall,

Humpty Dumpty had a great fall;

All the king's horses and all the king's men

Couldn't put Humpty together again.

fold here

SUGGESTION: Children may recite this poem in groups—one group saying the first two lines, and the other group saying the last two. Invite the group assigned to the first two lines to make paper puppets of a whole Humpty Dumpty and the wall. Ask the other group to make paper puppets of the king's horses and the king's men. Both groups can help make the broken pieces of Humpty Dumpty. When all the props are finished, have each group act out its assigned lines. Invite groups to switch so that each child acts out and recites the poem in its entirety.

I Can Do It Myself

Hat on head, just like this,

Pull it down, you see.

I can put my hat on

By myself, just me.

May be photocopied for classroom use. ©2018 by Irene C. Fountas and Gay Su Pinnell from *Sing a Song of Poetry, Kindergarten*. Portsmouth, NH: Heinemann.

ADDITIONAL VERSES:

One arm in, two arms in,

Buttons, one, two, three.

I can put my coat on

By myself, just me.

Toes in first, heels down next,

Pull and pull, then see—

I can put my boots on

By myself, just me.

Fingers here, thumbs right here,

Hands warm as can be.

I can put my mittens on

By myself, just me.

fold here

SUGGESTION: Perform this poem as a play with a different child acting out each verse using actual clothing (or just pantomiming putting on the garments). Make a shared writing list of things children can do by themselves, and invite them to illustrate it.

I Clap My Hands

I clap my hands,

I touch my feet,

I jump up from the ground.

I clap my hands,

I touch my feet,

And turn myself around.

SUGGESTION: Have children perform the actions of the poem as they repeat it two or three times. Later, have them look at a printed version of the poem and pick out simple words such as *I* and *my*.

fold here

I Clap My Hands to Make a Sound

I clap my hands to make a sound—

Clap, clap, clap!

I tap my toes to make a sound—

Tap, tap, tap!

I open my mouth to say a word—

Talk, talk, talk!

I pick up my foot to take a step—

Walk, walk, walk!

May be photocopied for classroom use. ©2018 by Irene C. Fountas and Gay Su Pinnell from *Sing a Song of Poetry, Kindergarten*. Portsmouth, NH: Heinemann.

fold here

SUGGESTION: Have children clap, tap, talk, and walk as they say this poem. Some of the class can be the audience while other children perform. Then reverse roles.

I Have a Little Wagon

I have a little wagon,

It goes all around the town.

I can pull it,

I can push it,

I can turn it upside down.

May be photocopied for classroom use. ©2018 by Irene C. Fountas and Gay Su Pinnell from *Sing a Song of Poetry, Kindergarten*. Portsmouth, NH: Heinemann.

ACTIONS:

I have a little wagon, [*hold hand out, palm up*]

It goes all around the town. [*move hand around*]

I can pull it, [*pull hand in*]

I can push it, [*push hand away*]

I can turn it upside down. [*turn hand upside down*]

SUGGESTION: After children chant and perform this action song, call attention to words that mean the opposite (*pull* and *push*) and rhyming words (*town* and *down*).

fold here

I Love Chocolate

I love chocolate

Yum, yum, yum.

I love chocolate

In my tum.

May be photocopied for classroom use. ©2018 by Irene C. Fountas and Gay Su Pinnell from *Sing a Song of Poetry, Kindergarten.* Portsmouth, NH: Heinemann.

fold here

SUGGESTION: Children will enjoy saying the poem over and over while eventually substituting their favorite foods. Have them clap the syllables of each new food. Eventually, use a printed version for shared reading.

I Measure Myself

I measure myself from my head to my toes,

I measure my arms, starting right by my nose,

I measure my legs, and I measure me all,

I measure to see if I'm growing tall.

SUGGESTION: After children learn the words, teach them movements to accompany each line: point from head to toe, point to nose and stretch out arms, point to length of legs, and then stretch out tall. Show children how to measure using a piece of yarn. They can work in partners to measure arms, legs, and so on. You can also read books about growing, such as *Titch* by Pat Hutchins (1993). Time permitting, invite children to talk about other ways they grow: e.g., how learning is a form of growing. Read *Leo the Late Bloomer* by Robert Kraus (1971), found in the *Fountas & Pinnell Classroom™ Interactive Read-Aloud Collection, Kindergarten* (2018) to accompany your class discussion.

fold here

I Scream

I scream.

You scream.

We all scream

For ice cream!

fold here

SUGGESTION: Compare the words *I scream* and *ice cream* while exaggerating and calling attention to the word breaks. Talk about how it helps to think about the meaning as you say the poem. Children can decorate a printed version of the poem with drawings of ice cream cones.

I Stand on Tiptoe

I stand on tiptoe

To make myself tall.

I bend my knees

To make myself small.

But I like my sitting size best of all!

SUGGESTION: This verse is another good stretch activity to use between activities. For each line of the rhyme, have children add movement: stand on toes, stretch, bend knees, crouch, and sit down. After the last line, children will all be sitting on the rug in front of you.

fold here

I Wiggle

I wiggle, wiggle, wiggle my fingers.

I wiggle, wiggle, wiggle my toes.

I wiggle, wiggle, wiggle my shoulders.

I wiggle, wiggle, wiggle my nose.

Now no more wiggles are left in me,

I am sitting as still as still can be.

May be photocopied for classroom use. ©2018 by Irene C. Fountas and Gay Su Pinnell from *Sing a Song of Poetry, Kindergarten*. Portsmouth, NH: Heinemann.

ACTIONS:

I wiggle, wiggle, wiggle my fingers. [*wiggle fingers*]

I wiggle, wiggle, wiggle my toes. [*wiggle toes*]

I wiggle, wiggle, wiggle my shoulders. [*wiggle shoulders*]

I wiggle, wiggle, wiggle my nose. [*wiggle nose*]

Now no more wiggles are left in me, [*shake head*]

I am sitting as still as still can be. [*sit still*]

fold here

SUGGESTION: The repetition of words and accompanying actions help children learn this poem. Revisit the poem throughout the day. It's a fun transition activity as the children gather for a read-aloud or other whole-class activity.

If I Were a Bird

If I were a bird,

I'd sing a song,

And fly about

The whole day long,

And when the night came,

Go to rest,

Up in my cozy little nest.

SUGGESTION: Assign different groups to read particular lines. You can create a beautiful version of the poem on chart paper by having children decorate the border with drawings of birds. The top of the chart can show birds flying, and the bottom can show birds on nests.

fold here

I'm a Choo-Choo Train

I'm a choo-choo train

Chugging down the track.

First I go forward,

Then I go back.

Now my bell is ringing,

Hear my whistle blow.

What a lot of noise I make

Everywhere I go!

ACTIONS:

I'm a choo-choo train [*bend arms at sides*]

Chugging down the track. [*rhythmically move arms*]

First I go forward, [*move forward*]

Then I go back. [*move backward*]

Now my bell is ringing, [*pretend to ring bell*]

Hear my whistle blow.

What a lot of noise I make [*cover ears*]

Everywhere I go!

May be photocopied for classroom use. ©2018 by Irene C. Fountas and Gay Su Pinnell from *Sing a Song of Poetry, Kindergarten*. Portsmouth, NH: Heinemann.

SUGGESTION: A whistle is a popular prop for this poem. Blow the whistle and have children take turns ringing a bell as the class pantomimes the poem together. Margaret Wise Brown's picture book, *Two Little Trains* (1977), and *Freight Train* by Donald Crews (1978) enrich the locomotive experience, particularly for children who are unfamiliar with trains. Additionally, invite children to talk about how trains are just one form of transportation after reading *Wheels on the Move* by Irene Quinn found in the *Fountas & Pinnell Classroom™ Shared Reading Collection, Kindergarten* (2018).

I'm Dusty Bill

I'm Dusty Bill

From Vinegar Hill.

Never had a bath

And I never will.

May be photocopied for classroom use. ©2018 by Irene C. Fountas and Gay Su Pinnell from *Sing a Song of Poetry, Kindergarten*. Portsmouth, NH: Heinemann.

SUGGESTION: Children will find this poem humorous. Invite them to recite the poem with expression and to say the last line louder than the other three.

fold here

I'm a Little Acorn Brown

I'm a little acorn brown,

Lying on the cold, cold ground.

Everyone walks over me,

That is why I'm cracked you see.

I'm a nut

In a rut.

I'm a nut

In a rut.

May be photocopied for classroom use. ©2018 by Irene C. Fountas and Gay Su Pinnell from *Sing a Song of Poetry, Kindergarten*. Portsmouth, NH: Heinemann.

fold here

SUGGESTION: Have children recite the poem while clapping their hands twice or snapping their fingers twice after each of the last four lines. Show them an acorn and explain that it is a seed from which a tree grows.

Jack and Jill

Jack and Jill went up the hill

To get a pail of water;

Jack fell down and broke his crown,

And Jill came tumbling after.

SUGGESTION: Children may be unfamiliar with what a well is, so take time to explain. Perhaps some of them have seen a well or drawn water from one. The meaning of the word *crown* in this poem may be confusing. Invite children to think about where kings and queens wear their crowns to help them figure out what part of the body the crown is. After they know the verse, have two children act out the parts as the rest of the class says it.

fold here

Jack, Be Nimble

Jack, be nimble,

Jack, be quick,

Jack, jump over

The candlestick.

SUGGESTION: Children enjoy discovering the meaning of the word *nimble*. Let them take turns jumping over a real or an imaginary candlestick, a set of blocks, or other low barrier. Each time, substitute the name of the child who is jumping. Alternatively, if you invite children to recite the poem outside, have them chant the words as they jump over a rope held by two of their classmates. If everyone makes it over one height, instruct children to raise the rope.

Jack-in-the-box

Jack-in-the-box,

Oh, so still.

Won't you come out?

Yes, I will.

ACTIONS:

Jack-in-the-box, [*tuck thumb in fist*]

Oh, so still. [*pause and stare at fist*]

Won't you come out? [*raise fist*]

Yes, I will. [*pop out thumb*]

fold here

SUGGESTION: Invite children to make simple pop-up puppets. Have them draw a jack-in-the-box character and cut it out, attach the puppet to a craft stick or straw, and then thread the straw or stick through a styrofoam cup with a hole in the bottom to hide the puppet. When it's time, instruct children to push up their straws so that their puppets pop out.

Jack, Jack

Jack, Jack, down you go,

Down in your box, down so low.

Jack, Jack, there goes the top,

Quickly now, up you pop!

SUGGESTION: Invite children to sit in a circle and repeatedly recite the poem while you turn the handle and wait for Jack to pop out of his box. With each new recitation, instruct them to substitute their names for Jack. When Jack finally pops out of his box, hand over the jack-in-the-box to the child whose name was, at the time, being recited. This child will take your place turning the handle while the rest of the class recites the poem until every child's name is used in place of Jack's.

Jack Sprat

Jack Sprat could eat no fat.

His wife could eat no lean.

And so between them both, you see,

They licked the platter clean.

May be photocopied for classroom use. ©2018 by Irene C. Fountas and Gay Su Pinnell from *Sing a Song of Poetry, Kindergarten*. Portsmouth, NH: Heinemann.

SUGGESTION: Assign a soloist for line 1, another soloist for line 2, and have the whole class read the final two lines. Introduce the idea of opposites, and help children think of some other examples like day and night, fast and slow, big and little, and so forth.

fold here

Jerry Hall

Jerry Hall,

He is so small,

A rat could eat him,

Hat and all.

May be photocopied for classroom use. ©2018 by Irene C. Fountas and Gay Su Pinnell from *Sing a Song of Poetry, Kindergarten*. Portsmouth, NH: Heinemann.

fold here

SUGGESTION: What would it be like to be very, very small? How would things look? Invite children to consider this and then work together to make a new version about a different person or animal with a different physical characteristic. A good book to use with this poem is *Mouse Views* by Bruce McMillan.

Johnny Taps with One Hammer

Johnny taps with one hammer,

One hammer, one hammer,

Johnny taps with one hammer,

Then he taps with two.

SUGGESTION: After children are familiar with the verse, they can add verses and change the numbers accordingly to practice counting up (or counting down for a more challenging recitation). Assign each child one verse and have him or her substitute his or her own name. After substituting for the number ten, instruct the child who's assigned to the final verse to end the poem by changing the last line to *Then he goes to bed.* Invite children to pantomime going to bed. Or purposely recite it before nap time.

fold here

Jumping Beans

One, two, three, four,

Beans came jumping through the door.

Five, six, seven, eight,

Jumping up onto my plate.

SUGGESTION: Children have a rollicking good time when they recite this poem and pretend to be jumping beans. Make a pretend doorway using two desk chairs. Position paper plates on the floor on one side of the door and ask children to line up outside the other. Invite them to jump through the door one at a time while reciting the poem. Instruct the first child to jump onto each plate until she or he lands on the last plate in line. Invite each child thereafter to follow suit until each jumping bean lands on her or his plate. After acting out the poem, have children take their plates back to their seats to draw accompanying illustrations.

Jumping Joan

Here I am, little jumping Joan.

When nobody's with me,

I'm always alone.

SUGGESTION: Have children draw themselves jumping. Arrange their drawings around the verse on a poetry chart. Discuss the idea that if no one is with you, then you are by yourself, or *alone*.

fold here

Ladybug! Ladybug!

Ladybug! Ladybug!

Fly away home.

Your house is on fire

And your children are gone.

All except one,

And that's little Ann,

For she has crept under

The frying pan.

May be photocopied for classroom use. ©2018 by Irene C. Fountas and Gay Su Pinnell from *Sing a Song of Poetry, Kindergarten*. Portsmouth, NH: Heinemann.

fold here

SUGGESTION: Have children substitute other rhyming words for *Ann* and *frying pan*: e.g., *Joan* and *telephone*. Eric Carle's book, *The Grouchy Ladybug*, is a fun read that also features a ladybug.

Lazy Mary

Lazy Mary,

Will you get up,

Will you get up,

Will you get up?

Lazy Mary,

Will you get up

This cold and frosty morning?

No, no mother,

I won't get up,

I won't get up,

I won't get up.

No, no mother,

I won't get up.

This cold and frosty morning.

SUGGESTION: Substitute other names as well as other words like *yes* and *I will* for *no* and *I won't*. Also try substituting *cold* and *frosty* for other weather conditions. How many weather words can children think of? Invite them to make a shared writing list.

fold here

151

Little Ball

A little ball,

A bigger ball,

A great big ball I see.

Shall we count them?

Are you ready?

One,

Two,

Three.

fold here

SUGGESTION: While chanting the poem, have children use actions to indicate the three ball sizes by making a circle with a finger and thumb, with hands, and then with arms.

Little Bo-Peep

Little Bo-Peep has lost her sheep,

And doesn't know where to find them.

Leave them alone and they'll come home,

Wagging their tails behind them.

SUGGESTION: Divide children into two groups, and assign the first two lines to one group and the last two lines to the other. Invite children to recite the first two lines sadly and the last two lines joyfully. Have a discussion about the story this poem tells.

fold here

A Little Doggie

A little doggie,

All brown and black,

Wore his tail

Curled on his back.

May be photocopied for classroom use. ©2018 by Irene C. Fountas and Gay Su Pinnell from *Sing a Song of Poetry, Kindergarten.* Portsmouth, NH: Heinemann.

fold here

SUGGESTION: This description of a little doggie is fun for children to draw and share. Have them invent other doggie details. Display the children's drawings around the printed poem on a poetry chart.

Little Jack Horner

Little Jack Horner

Sat in a corner,

Eating his holiday pie;

He put in his thumb

And pulled out a plum,

And said, "What a good boy am I!"

May be photocopied for classroom use. ©2018 by Irene C. Fountas and Gay Su Pinnell from *Sing a Song of Poetry, Kindergarten*. Portsmouth, NH: Heinemann.

SUGGESTION: Invite children to take turns being Jack (or Jackie). Children will have a lot to say about why Jack is eating pie with his thumb. And they may have lots of ideas about a holiday pie. What could it be? Have children draw, dictate, and write their ideas. These recipes are fun to share.

fold here

Little Jack Sprat

Little Jack Sprat

Once had a pig.

It was not very little,

It was not very big.

It was not very lean,

It was not very fat.

"It's a good pig to grunt,"

Said little Jack Sprat.

May be photocopied for classroom use. ©2018 by Irene C. Fountas and Gay Su Pinnell from *Sing a Song of Poetry, Kindergarten*. Portsmouth, NH: Heinemann.

fold here

SUGGESTION: Children will enjoy this variation, particularly if they already know the traditional verse (see "Jack Sprat" in this volume). Point out that *grunt* is a word for the sound pigs make. Discuss words in the poem that are opposites.

Little Miss Muffet

Little Miss Muffet

Sat on a tuffet,

Eating her curds and whey;

Along came a spider,

Who sat down beside her,

And frightened Miss Muffet away!

SUGGESTION: This poem tells a story that can be acted out. Children may also like to talk about if they like spiders or are scared of them. They may be interested to learn that *curds and whey* is similar to cottage cheese.

fold here

Little Miss Tucket

Little Miss Tucket

Sat on a bucket,

Eating her peaches and cream;

There came a grasshopper

Who tried hard to stop her

But she said, "Go away or I'll scream!"

fold here

SUGGESTION: Once children know the poem "Little Miss Muffet," they will find this variation amusing. Invite them to create other variations by substituting out the words *tucket* and *bucket*: e.g., *Little Miss Pox / Sat on a box.*

Little Mouse

Walk little mouse, walk little mouse.

Hide little mouse, hide little mouse.

Here comes the cat!

Run little mouse, run little mouse!

SUGGESTION: Have children accompany the verse with actions: tiptoe around, cover eyes with hands, look around, and run away. Or invite children to act out the story; lots of mice and one cat equals a creative outside activity. Children can also substitute *walk*, *hide*, and *run* with other action words like *crawl*, *kneel*, and *skip*.

fold here

Little Paul Parrot

Little Paul Parrot

Sat in his garret,

Eating toast and tea;

A little brown mouse

Jumped into the house,

And stole the toast for me.

May be photocopied for classroom use. ©2018 by Irene C. Fountas and Gay Su Pinnell from *Sing a Song of Poetry, Kindergarten*. Portsmouth, NH: Heinemann.

SUGGESTION: Invite two children, one playing the parrot and the other the mouse, to act out the rhyme as the group says it. While children tell the story of the poem, explain how a *garret* is similar to an attic or top floor.

Little Pup

Little pup, little pup,

What do you say?

"Woof, woof, woof!

Let's go and play."

ADDITIONAL VERSES:

Kittycat, kittycat,

How about you?

"Meow, meow, meow!

And I purr, too."

Pretty bird, pretty bird,

Have you a song?

"Tweet, tweet, tweet!

The whole day long."

Jersey cow, jersey cow,

What do you do?

"Moo, moo, moo!

And give milk, too."

Little lamb, little lamb,

What do you say?

"Baa, baa, baa!

Can Mary play?"

May be photocopied for classroom use. ©2018 by Irene C. Fountas and Gay Su Pinnell from *Sing a Song of Poetry, Kindergarten*. Portsmouth, NH: Heinemann.

SUGGESTION: Recite this poem as a game. Have one child recite the first rhymed question and choose a classmate to answer it. This child then chooses someone to ask the next question. Begin with one or two animals used over and over, but expand as children learn more verses. Children who are chosen have to pick up the cue from the first two lines and respond as the appropriate animal.

fold here

Little Red Apple

A little red apple grew high in a tree.

I looked up at it.

It looked down at me.

"Come down, please," I said.

And that little red apple fell right on my head.

May be photocopied for classroom use. ©2018 by Irene C. Fountas and Gay Su Pinnell from *Sing a Song of Poetry, Kindergarten*. Portsmouth, NH: Heinemann.

ACTIONS:

A little red apple grew high in a tree. [*point up*]

I looked up at it. [*shade eyes and look up*]

It looked down at me. [*shade eyes and look down*]

"Come down, please," I said. [*motion downward*]

And that little red apple fell right on my head. [*tap top of head*]

SUGGESTION: Teach children this verse and the finger and hand movements that go along with it. They can also talk about the story the poem tells and discuss if an apple can really look down. They may conclude that the speaker is wishing for an apple and one happens to fall.

Little Snail

The snail is so slow,

The snail is so slow.

He creeps along

And creeps along.

The snail is

So-o s-l-o-w.

SUGGESTION: Sing this verse to the tune of "The Farmer in the Dell," or simply recite it, saying the last two words very, very slowly.

fold here

Little Tommy Tucker

Little Tommy Tucker sings for his supper.

What shall he sing for?

White bread and butter.

How shall he cut it without any knife?

How shall he marry without any wife?

fold here

SUGGESTION: Invite children to consider what it means for a child to *sing for his supper* and how he can cut bread without a knife. Children will enjoy trying to unravel these mysteries.

Little White Rabbit

Little white rabbit,

Hop on one foot, one foot.

Little white rabbit,

Hop on two feet, two feet.

Little white rabbit,

Hop on three feet, three feet.

Little white rabbit,

Hop on four feet, four feet.

Little white rabbit,

Hop, hop, hop.

May be photocopied for classroom use. ©2018 by Irene C. Fountas and Gay Su Pinnell from *Sing a Song of Poetry, Kindergarten.* Portsmouth, NH: Heinemann.

SUGGESTION: This poem is a good counting rhyme. Children can substitute other colors in place of *white*. Also invite them to substitute for other hopping or jumping animals: e.g., a *kangaroo*, a *frog*, or a *spider*. Ask children to think about how some animals hop or jump on two feet, while others may hop or jump on four or even eight feet. Have children read their variations according to each new animal's number of feet.

fold here

London Bridge

London Bridge is falling down,

Falling down, falling down,

London Bridge is falling down,

My fair lady.

May be photocopied for classroom use. ©2018 by Irene C. Fountas and Gay Su Pinnell from *Sing a Song of Poetry, Kindergarten.* Portsmouth, NH: Heinemann.

ADDITIONAL VERSES:

Build it up with wood and clay,
Wood and clay, wood and clay,
Build it up with wood and clay,
My fair lady.

Wood and clay will wash away,
Wash away, wash away,
Wood and clay will wash away,
My fair lady.

Build it up with iron bars,
Iron bars, iron bars,
Build it up with iron bars,
My fair lady.

Iron bars will bend and break,
Bend and break, bend and break,
Iron bars will bend and break,
My fair lady.

SUGGESTION: Play a game in which two children form a bridge by joining their hands, both arms stretched upward. Ask the other children to march under the arch in single file as they sing the song. On *My fair lady*, the arch falls, capturing a child, who becomes an observer. Continue until all children have been caught.

The Lost Shoe

Doodle, doodle, do,

The princess lost her shoe.

Her highness hopped,

The fiddler stopped,

Not knowing what to do.

May be photocopied for classroom use. ©2018 by Irene C. Fountas and Gay Su Pinnell from *Sing a Song of Poetry, Kindergarten*. Portsmouth, NH: Heinemann.

SUGGESTION: Have children demonstrate how you might hop on one foot if you lost a shoe. Explain to children that *her highness* is what you might call a princess.

fold here

Lucy Locket

Lucy Locket lost her pocket,

Kitty Fisher found it;

Not a penny was there in it,

Only ribbon 'round it.

fold here

SUGGESTION: Emphasize the meter by tapping a rhythm stick while the children say the poem. Have two groups take turns reading every other line; one group says the first and third lines, and the other responds with the second and fourth lines. Explain that a *pocket* in this poem is a "purse" or a "pocketbook."

Make a Pancake

Make a pancake, pat, pat, pat.

Do not make it fat, fat, fat.

You must make it flat, flat, flat.

Make a pancake just like that.

fold here

SUGGESTION: Have children perform actions as they say the rhyme: pat hands together, stretch hands apart, pat hands together, and clap hands. Print the words to this rhyme on a poetry chart and read and illustrate the poem together. Or prepare pocket chart strips and invite children to put them in order to recreate the poem. Once children know the poem, give them a printed version so they can notice and highlight the -*at* phonogram.

Mary, Mary, Quite Contrary

Mary, Mary, quite contrary,

How does your garden grow?

With silver bells and cockleshells,

And pretty maids all in a row.

fold here

SUGGESTION: What does it mean to be *contrary*? Have children discuss this concept and talk about when they have acted this way. Tell children that *silver bells* are a kind of flower and *cockleshells* are marine mollusks, and ask them what they think they are doing in the poem's garden. Substitute children's names for *Mary*.

Mix a Pancake

by Christina Rosetti

Mix a pancake,

Stir a pancake,

Pop it in the pan;

Fry the pancake,

Toss the pancake—

Catch it if you can.

SUGGESTION: This is a great poem for children to pantomime mixing, stirring, popping, frying, tossing, and catching pancakes. This poem pairs well with Tomie dePaola's wordless picture book, *Pancakes for Breakfast* (1978), in which children enjoy predicting what happens next.

fold here

The Mocking Bird

Hush, little baby, don't say a word,

Papa's going to buy you a mocking bird.

If the mocking bird won't sing,

Papa's going to buy you a diamond ring.

If the diamond ring turns to brass,

Papa's going to buy you a looking glass.

If the looking glass gets broke,

Papa's going to buy you a billy goat.

If that billy goat runs away,

Papa's going to buy you a bale of hay.

May be photocopied for classroom use. ©2018 by Irene C. Fountas and Gay Su Pinnell from *Sing a Song of Poetry, Kindergarten*. Portsmouth, NH: Heinemann.

fold here

SUGGESTION: Sing this song together as a class. Some children may need help with the vocabulary *mocking bird*, *looking glass*, *billy goat*, and *bale of hay*. Ask them to help you create additional verses to this lullaby.

The Muffin Man

Oh, do you know the muffin man,

The muffin man, the muffin man?

Oh, do you know the muffin man

Who lives in Drury Lane?

Oh, yes, I know the muffin man,

The muffin man, the muffin man.

Oh, yes, I know the muffin man

Who lives in Drury Lane.

fold here

SUGGESTION: Have one group of children sing the first verse and another group sing the second verse. When all the children are familiar with the words, turn this into a game full of suspense; blindfold one class member, have the class sing the first verse, point to one child to sing the second verse as a solo, and give the blindfolded child three guesses to name the soloist. When the soloist is named, blindfold him or her and continue the game.

My Dog, Rags

I have a dog and his name is Rags,

He eats so much that his tummy sags,

His ears flip-flop and his tail wig-wags,

And when he walks he zig-zig-zags!

May be photocopied for classroom use. ©2018 by Irene C. Fountas and Gay Su Pinnell from *Sing a Song of Poetry, Kindergarten*. Portsmouth, NH: Heinemann.

ACTIONS:

I have a dog and his name is Rags, [*point to self*]

He eats so much that his tummy sags, [*put hands together in front of stomach*]

His ears flip-flop and his tail wig-wags, [*bend each hand at wrist*]

And when he walks he zig-zig-zags! [*make an imaginary Z with index finger*]

fold here

SUGGESTION: Have children learn the words of this verse and the motions to accompany it. If you are using a printed version, call attention to the phonogram -*ag* with the plural -*s*.

My Eyes Can See

My eyes can see.

My mouth can talk.

My ears can hear.

My feet can walk.

My nose can sniff.

My teeth can chew.

My eyelids can blink.

My arms can hug you.

SUGGESTION: Children will naturally want to act out the words being said. You can use a drawing of a person with this poem and point to the parts of the body.

fold here

My Head

This is the circle that is my head.

This is my mouth with which words are said.

These are my eyes with which I see.

This is my nose that is part of me.

This is the hair that grows on my head,

And this is my hat I wear on my head.

May be photocopied for classroom use. ©2018 by Irene C. Fountas and Gay Su Pinnell from *Sing a Song of Poetry, Kindergarten.* Portsmouth, NH: Heinemann.

SUGGESTION: Have children point to or otherwise indicate on their own faces each feature as it is mentioned. You can also use an enlarged drawing or a photo of a face. Alternatively, invite children to draw self-portraits with the characteristics of the poem and label them.

My Little Sister

My little sister dressed in pink

Washed all the dishes in the sink.

How many dishes did she break?

One, two, three, four, five.

SUGGESTION: Help children acquire their vocabulary by coming up with variations like *My little brother dressed in blue / Washed all the animals at the zoo*. Ask children to count to five on their fingers or to hop once on *one*, twice on *two*, and so on.

fold here

Old MacDonald Had a Farm

Old MacDonald had a farm,

E - I - E - I - O

And on this farm he had a cow,

E - I - E - I - O

With a moo, moo here,

And a moo, moo there,

Here a moo, there a moo,

Everywhere a moo, moo,

Old MacDonald had a farm,

E - I - E - I - O.

SUGGESTION: Teach the song, and then have children add more verses featuring other animals and the noises they make: *pig—oink, oink; cat—meow, meow; dog—bow-wow;* and *horse—neigh, neigh.* Accompany the verses with motions representative of the different animals. Make each verse cumulative, repeating all the animal noises each time. Sing a version of the song in which the farm owner is female: *Mom MacDonald had a farm.* Follow up by reading *Ms. MacDonald Has a Class* by Jan Ormerod (1996), or *Old MacDonald* adapted by Lisa Lopez found in the *Fountas & Pinnell Classroom™ Shared Reading Collection, Kindergarten* (2018).

Oliver Twist

Oliver Twist, can you do this?

If so, do so.

Number one, touch your tongue.

Number two, touch your shoe.

Number three, touch your knee.

Number four, touch the floor.

Number five, jump up high.

May be photocopied for classroom use. ©2018 by Irene C. Fountas and Gay Su Pinnell from *Sing a Song of Poetry, Kindergarten*. Portsmouth, NH: Heinemann.

SUGGESTION: Once children are familiar with the rhyme, have them work with a partner. One partner recites the poem and the other performs the actions. Then have the partners switch roles. Invite children to come up with their own actions for Oliver Twist to do.

fold here

One Potato, Two Potato

One potato, two potato,

Three potato, four,

Five potato, six potato,

Seven potato more,

Eight potato, nine potato,

Where is ten?

Now we must count over again.

May be photocopied for classroom use. ©2018 by Irene C. Fountas and Gay Su Pinnell from *Sing a Song of Poetry, Kindergarten*. Portsmouth, NH: Heinemann.

SUGGESTION: Have children make two fists and alternate tapping one on top of the other as they recite this rhyme. The rhyme can also be used in a counting game. Have children stand in a circle with one player in the middle. The children in the circle hold out two fists each. The player in the middle taps alternate fists, in sequence, each time she or he says a number word or the word *more*. Tapped fists go behind backs. The winner is the last player to have both fists eliminated.

One, Two, Buckle My Shoe

One, two,

Buckle my shoe.

Three, four,

Knock at the door.

Five, six,

Pick up sticks.

Seven, eight,

Lay them straight.

Nine, ten,

A big fat hen.

SUGGESTION: This is an easy counting rhyme with specific motions that can be pantomimed for each pair of numbers. After children know the rhyme, write it on a chart using numerals in place of the number words. You may want to make a big book with five pages—one for every pair of lines—or five-page little books for children to illustrate.

fold here

One, Two, Three, Four

One, two, three, four

Mary's at the cottage door,

Five, six, seven, eight,

Eating cherries off a plate.

fold here

SUGGESTION: Have one group chant the first and third lines and a second group respond with the alternate lines. Substitute children's names for *Mary*. Invite a child to act out the line *Eating cherries off a plate*.

Open, Shut Them

Open, shut them,

Open, shut them,

Give a little clap.

Open, shut them.

Open, shut them.

ADDITIONAL VERSES:

Creep them, creep them,
Creep them, creep them,
Right up to your chin.
Open up your mouth.
But do not let them in.

Roll them, roll them,
Roll them, roll them,
To your shoulders fly.
Then like little birdies,
Let them flutter to the sky.

Faster, faster,
Faster, faster,
Give a little clap.
Slower, slower, slower, slower,
Lay them in your lap.

Crawl them, crawl them,
Crawl them, crawl them,
Give a little shriek.
And through your fingers peek.

Falling, falling,
Falling, falling,
Right down to the ground.
Quickly pick them up again,
And turn them 'round and 'round.

May be photocopied for classroom use. ©2018 by Irene C. Fountas and Gay Su Pinnell from *Sing a Song of Poetry, Kindergarten*. Portsmouth, NH: Heinemann.

SUGGESTION: Children will enjoy the hand movements of the actions in this poem: opening and shutting both hands to clap, creeping them up to their chins and then eyes, rolling them and fluttering them high, and then letting them fall to the ground before laying them in their laps.

fold here

Pat-a-cake

Pat-a-cake, pat-a-cake, baker's man,

Bake me a cake as fast as you can.

Pat it and prick it and mark it with *B*,

And put it in the oven for Tommy and me.

SUGGESTION: Have children recite this rhyme in pairs. For the first two lines, instruct them to pat their hands on their thighs, clap their hands together at chest level, and then put their hands out with palms up to pat their partner's hands. For line 3, mime patting, pricking, and writing a *B* in the air. For line 4, mime putting the cake in the oven and then pretend to cradle a baby back and forth.

A Peanut Sat on a Railroad Track

A peanut sat on a railroad track,

Its heart was all a-flutter.

Around the bend

Came Number Ten.

Toot! Toot! Peanut butter!

fold here

SUGGESTION: *Toot! Toot!* is just one sound the train can make as it comes down the railroad track. Children can incorporate other sound effects, such as a bell, tambourine, whistle, and even other word like *chooo-chooo*, *ch-ch-ch-ch*, and *whooo-oo-oo-ooo*. Motions can show a heart *all a-flutter* and the approaching train. For a grand finale, children can smash their hands together on *Peanut butter!*

Peas

I eat my peas with honey,

I've done it all my life.

It makes the peas taste funny,

But it keeps them on the knife.

May be photocopied for classroom use. ©2018 by Irene C. Fountas and Gay Su Pinnell from *Sing a Song of Poetry, Kindergarten*. Portsmouth, NH: Heinemann.

fold here

SUGGESTION: This poem conjures up a comical image: peas balanced on a knife. Have children draw a picture of this or act it out. Replace *peas* with other foods that are hard to balance on a knife, such as grapes. As they become familiar with the structure of the rhyme, ask them to try to create verses about other food items and/or eating utensils. (See "Beets" in this volume.)

Pease Porridge Hot

Pease porridge hot,

Pease porridge cold,

Pease porridge in the pot,

Nine days old.

Some like it hot,

Some like it cold,

Some like it in the pot,

Nine days old.

ACTIONS:

Pease porridge hot, [*clap own hands*]

Pease porridge cold, [*clap partner's hands*]

Pease porridge in the pot, [*clap own hands*]

Nine days old. [*clap partner's hands*]

Some like it hot, [*one fist on top of the other*]

Some like it cold, [*alternate fists, placing the other on top*]

Some like it in the pot, [*clap partner's hands*]

Nine days old. [*clap own hands*]

SUGGESTION: This is a snappy, clappy poem! Have children perform the actions, or have them divide into two groups to recite and perform alternate lines or alternate stanzas.

fold here

Peter, Peter, Pumpkin-eater

Peter, Peter, pumpkin-eater,

Had a wife and couldn't keep her.

He put her in a pumpkin shell,

And there he kept her very well.

May be photocopied for classroom use. ©2018 by Irene C. Fountas and Gay Su Pinnell from *Sing a Song of Poetry, Kindergarten*. Portsmouth, NH: Heinemann.

fold here

SUGGESTION: What is a *pumpkin-eater*, and what does one have to do with the poem? What would it be like to live in a pumpkin house? A pumpkin-shell home is a fun image for children to draw.

Point to the Right

Point to the right of me.

Point to the left of me.

Point up above me.

Point down below.

Right, left, up,

And down so slow.

SUGGESTION: Have children use both arms to point in the directions indicated. Emphasize saying the poem with expression while slowing down on the last line.

fold here

Puppies and Kittens

One little, two little, three little kittens

Were napping in the sun.

One little, two little, three little puppies

Said, "Let's have some fun."

Up to the kittens the puppies went creeping,

As quiet as could be.

One little, two little, three little kittens

Went scampering up a tree!

ACTIONS:

One little, two little, three little kittens [*pop up three fingers*]
Were napping in the sun. [*rest head on hands*]
One little, two little, three little puppies [*pop up three fingers*]
Said, "Let's have some fun." [*smile*]

Up to the kittens the puppies went creeping, [*creep right fingers up left arm*]
As quiet as could be. [*hold an index finger up to lips*]
One little, two little, three little kittens [*pop up three fingers*]
Went scampering up a tree! [*wiggle fingers overhead*]

fold here

SUGGESTION: The great vocabulary in this poem—*napping, creeping, scampering*—can be reinforced by miming the actions.

Pussycat, Pussycat

"Pussycat, pussycat, where have you been?"

"I've been to London to visit the Queen!"

"Pussycat, pussycat, what did you do there?"

"I frightened a little mouse under her chair."

May be photocopied for classroom use. ©2018 by Irene C. Fountas and Gay Su Pinnell from *Sing a Song of Poetry, Kindergarten.* Portsmouth, NH: Heinemann.

SUGGESTION: Learn the verse as a whole group, and then have one group of children read the questions and the others respond. Or children can recite it with a partner. If you are using a printed version of the poem, you may want to point out the use of quotation marks. Ask children if they have noticed quotation marks in books you've read together, and discuss what they mean.

fold here

Rain on the Rooftops

Rain on the rooftops,

Rain on the trees,

Rain on the green grass,

But not on me!

fold here

SUGGESTION: After children learn this verse, they will enjoy thinking of imaginative places it could rain and making their own rhymes. Substitute other words for *rain*, such as *snow, hail, sleet,* or *sunshine.*

Rain, Rain, Go Away

Rain, rain, go away,

Come again another day.

Rain, rain, go away.

Little _____ wants to play.

May be photocopied for classroom use. ©2018 by Irene C. Fountas and Gay Su Pinnell from *Sing a Song of Poetry, Kindergarten.* Portsmouth, NH: Heinemann.

fold here

SUGGESTION: Personalize the poem by inserting the name of someone in the class. Have children make gentle rain sounds by rubbing their hands together or lightly tapping on desks or tables. Make a photocopy of the verse for everyone in the class and let them write in their own names. (Later they can take the poem home and recite it to family members.) Help children create their own variation of the poem, such as: *Rain, rain, go away, / Because we want a snow day.*

Red, White, and Blue

Red, white, and blue,

Tap me on the shoe.

Red, white, and green,

Tap me on the bean.

Red, white, and black,

Tap me on the back.

SUGGESTION: One way to help children memorize poems and songs is by using the echo technique: say a line, have children repeat it, and after every two or three lines have them say everything they've learned so far. Have children perform the motions as they say the words of this poem. Explain that *tap me on the bean* means "tap me on the head." Invite them to create new verses using different colors and rhyming words like *red/head* and *brown/frown*.

Ride a Cockhorse to Banbury Cross

Ride a cockhorse

To Banbury Cross,

To see a fine lady

Upon a white horse;

Rings on her fingers

And bells on her toes,

She shall have music

Wherever she goes.

fold here

SUGGESTION: The words and rhythm of this poem mimic the sound of hoofbeats. Let children mark the beat by clapping their hands or tapping their feet. Have different groups read each line. Children can imagine how the fine lady would look with rings on her fingers and bells on her toes. Invite them to illustrate the image.

Rig-a-jig-jig

Thumbkin, pointer, middleman big,

Silly man, wee man,

Rig-a-jig-jig.

fold here

SUGGESTION: Have children touch the appropriate digit on each hand together as they name it and then roll their hands around as they say *rig-a-jig-jig.*

Ring Around the Rosie

Ring around the rosie,

A pocket full of posies,

Ashes! Ashes!

We all fall down.

SUGGESTION: Have children join hands in a circle and walk in one direction as they say the words. The exciting highlight of this game comes with the words *all fall down*; everyone sits down on the floor! Invite children to chant the verse again while walking in the reverse direction.

fold here

The Rooster

Cock-a-doodle-do!

The rooster flaps his wings,

Cock-a-doodle-do!

He flaps his wings and sings,

Cock-a-doodle-do!

The rooster sings and then,

Cock-a-doodle-do!

Cock-a-doodle-do!

He flaps his wings again.

fold here

SUGGESTION: Use sounds from simple instruments such as a xylophone or tambourine to accompany the repetition of the sound *Cock-a-doodle-do!*

Roses Are Red

Roses are red,

Violets are blue,

Sugar is sweet,

And so are you.

fold here

SUGGESTION: See how many other kinds of flowers the class can name. Make new versions of the poem using other categories, colors, and descriptions like *Tomatoes are red, / Blueberries are blue, / Corn is yellow, / Violets for you.* Time permitting, read books about colors from the *Fountas & Pinnell Classroom™ Interactive Read-Aloud Collection, Kindergarten* (2018): e.g., Stephen R. Swinburne's *What Color Is Nature?* (2002), Jane Cabrera's *Cat's Colors* (2000), Roseanne Thong's *Red Is a Dragon* (2008), or Emma Dodd's *Dog's Colorful Day: A Messy Story About Colors and Counting* (2003).

Row, Row, Row Your Boat

Row, row, row your boat

Gently down the stream;

Merrily, merrily, merrily, merrily,

Life is but a dream.

Row, row, row your boat

Down the jungle stream;

If you see a crocodile,

Don't forget to scream!

May be photocopied for classroom use. ©2018 by Irene C. Fountas and Gay Su Pinnell from *Sing a Song of Poetry, Kindergarten*. Portsmouth, NH: Heinemann.

SUGGESTION: Have children sing this song as they mime rowing. When they know the song well, they can sing it as a round. The first group starts singing (and keeps going), the second group begins when the first finishes the second line. Invite children to try variations like *Rock, rock, rock your boat / Gently to and fro; / Watch out! Give a shout, / In the water you go!*

Sally, Go 'Round

Sally, go 'round the sun,

Sally, go 'round the moon,

Sally, go 'round the chimney pots

Every afternoon.

BUMP!

SUGGESTION: See John and Nancy Langstaff's book *Sally Go 'Round the Moon* for the music to this and similar songs. Children love to spin as they say this rhyme and to reverse the direction of their spin on the poem's last line. Alternatively, invite them to make a circle and skip to the left before reversing the direction of their skip when they say *Bump!*

fold here

See-Saw, Marjorie Daw

See-saw, Marjorie Daw,

Jack will have a new master;

He shall have but a penny a day,

Because he won't work any faster.

SUGGESTION: This poem's meaning is unclear (a different version reads: *See-saw, Marjorie Daw, / Sold her bed and lay upon straw*), but there's magic in saying it together and enjoying the way the words rhyme. Have children make up their own stories about Marjorie Daw and Jack.

Sing, Sing

Sing, sing,

What will I sing?

The cat ran away

With the pudding string!

Do, do,

What will I do?

The cat ran away

With the pudding, too!

SUGGESTION: Children may have difficulty understanding how pudding (which to them is a dessert) could have a string. Explain that in olden times, pudding was a sausage (like a hot dog) with a string at the end. Invite them to think about why a cat would run away with pudding.

fold here

Slippery Soap

Slippery, slippery, slippery soap!

Now you see it, now you don't.

Slide it on your arms, one, two, three,

Now your arms are slippery!

Slide it on your legs, one, two, three,

Now your legs are slippery!

SUGGESTION: The beginning letters in the words *slippery soap* might be thought to sound slippery and slick. Invite children to say *slippery* quickly and slowly: *slip-per-y*. Have them pantomime imaginary soap bars slipping out of their hands as they recite the first line of the poem. Sliding, slithering actions will come naturally as they manipulate the invisible soap bars around their arms sand legs. Have them repeat the rhyme, inserting different parts of the body: *toes, knees, knuckles, elbows, ankles*. If they insert a singular body part, like *neck*, remind them to change the verb to the singular *is*.

A Small Caterpillar

"Who's that tickling my back?"

Said the wall.

"Me," said a small caterpillar,

"I'm learning to crawl."

SUGGESTION: This poem has a surprise point of view; a wall asks the question and the caterpillar answers. Cover up the word *caterpillar* in both the title and the third line. Then divide the class into two groups; assign one group to read for the (unknown) caterpillar and the other for the wall. Ask children to think about what could be *tickling* a wall. Allow them to guess. If needed, give more clues: e.g., *it's an insect*. Finally, reveal the answer. Afterward, try reciting variations of this poem using the other animals children guessed.

Snail, Snail

Snail, snail,

Put out your horns,

And I'll give you bread

And barleycorns.

May be photocopied for classroom use. ©2018 by Irene C. Fountas and Gay Su Pinnell from *Sing a Song of Poetry, Kindergarten*. Portsmouth, NH: Heinemann.

SUGGESTION: While reciting the poem, have children create a snail by making a fist, thumb tucked inside, and then lifting the little finger and index finger to make the horns.

Someone's Birthday

Today is a birthday,

I wonder for whom.

We know it's somebody

Who's right in this room.

So look all around you

For somebody who

Is laughing and smiling

My goodness—it's you!

May be photocopied for classroom use. ©2018 by Irene C. Fountas and Gay Su Pinnell from *Sing a Song of Poetry, Kindergarten*. Portsmouth, NH: Heinemann.

SUGGESTION: After reading the poem, place a special hat or button on the child whose birthday it is. Invite the birthday child to choose a story for the group read-aloud.

fold here

Sometimes

Sometimes I am tall,

Sometimes I am small.

Sometimes I am very, very, tall,

Sometimes I am very, very, small.

Sometimes tall,

Sometimes small.

Sometimes neither tall nor small.

SUGGESTION: Have children act out the rhyme: stand tall, crouch low, stand on tiptoes, crouch and lower head, stand tall, crouch down, and then stand straight. Teach measurement in connection with this chant. Measure the children at the beginning of the school year and record their heights on a chart; then measure and record their heights again midyear and, finally, once more at the end of the year so that children see real evidence of *small* and *tall*.

Stop, Look, and Listen

Stop, look, and listen

Before you cross the street.

First use your eyes and ears,

Then use your feet.

SUGGESTION: After children learn this poem, have them add hand and foot movements. For the first line, they *stop* by raising their hand out in front of them as if they were stopping traffic, turn their heads left and right to *look* both ways, and then cup one ear with their hands to *listen*. For the second line, they hold one arm out, palm down and elbow bent, and use two fingers of the other hand to indicate a walking motion across the outstretched arm. For the third line, they hold up one finger to indicate *first* and use that same finger to point to their eyes and ears. They then walk in place for the final line.

fold here

Stretch

Stretch to the windows,

Stretch to the door,

Stretch up to the ceiling,

And bend to the floor.

SUGGESTION: Have children perform the stated actions as they chant the words by pointing to areas in the classroom (window, door, ceiling, floor).

Stretching Fun

I stretch and stretch and find it fun

To try to reach up to the sun.

I bend and bend to touch the ground,

Then I twist and twist around.

May be photocopied for classroom use. ©2018 by Irene C. Fountas and Gay Su Pinnell from *Sing a Song of Poetry, Kindergarten*. Portsmouth, NH: Heinemann.

SUGGESTION: Children get some good stretching exercise as they say the rhyme and perform the stated actions. Have children say *stretch* and *touch* or *ground* and *around* to notice that they have the same ending sounds.

Teddy Bear, Teddy Bear

Teddy bear, teddy bear,
Turn around.

Teddy bear, teddy bear,
Touch the ground.

Teddy bear, teddy bear,
Touch your shoe.

Teddy bear, teddy bear,
Say howdy-do.

Teddy bear, teddy bear,
Turn out the light.

Teddy bear, teddy bear,
Say good night.

fold here

SUGGESTION: Have children perform the actions in this poem. Repetition of the first line helps children learn the verses. Alternatively, have children make up their own verses and actions.

Teeter-totter

Teeter-totter, bread and water,

I'll be the son and you be the daughter.

Teeter-totter, bread and water,

I'll eat the bread and you drink the water.

SUGGESTION: Have children pair up and imitate the up-and-down motion of the teeter-totter as they say the poem.

fold here

Ten Little Fingers

I have ten little fingers,

And they all belong to me.

I can make them do things.

Do you want to see?

I can make them point,

I can make them hold,

I can make them dance,

And then I make them fold.

ACTIONS:

I have ten little fingers, [*hold up ten fingers*]

And they all belong to me. [*point to self*]

I can make them do things. [*wiggle fingers*]

Do you want to see? [*tilt head*]

I can make them point, [*point*]

I can make them hold, [*hold fingertips together*]

I can make them dance, [*dance fingers on arm*]

And then I make them fold. [*fold hands in lap*]

fold here

SUGGESTION: Have children perform the actions indicated above. They can end by counting all ten fingers and then folding them again.

There Once Was a Queen

There once was a queen

Whose face was green.

She ate her milk

And drank her bread,

And got up in the morning

To go to bed.

May be photocopied for classroom use. ©2018 by Irene C. Fountas and Gay Su Pinnell from *Sing a Song of Poetry, Kindergarten*. Portsmouth, NH: Heinemann.

SUGGESTION: Invite children to discuss what makes this poem funny. What words would they change to make it not funny?

fold here

There Was an Old Woman

There was an old woman,

Who lived under a hill.

And if she's not gone,

She lives there still.

SUGGESTION: Help children understand the last two lines of the poem. (A different way to say those two lines is that the old woman is still living there.) Invite them to say the lines of the poem quickly while clapping at the rhyming words *hill* and *still*.

There Was an Old Woman Who Lived in a Shoe

There was an old woman

Who lived in a shoe,

She had so many children

She didn't know what to do.

She gave them some soup

With butter and bread,

Kissed them all fondly

And put them to bed.

SUGGESTION: Create a written version of this familiar verse and illustrate it with a large shoe. You can put small photos of the children in the shoe or have them draw and cut out pictures of themselves. They will enjoy taking turns reading the poem with a pointer after they know it.

fold here

This Is the Way We Go to School

This is the way we go to school,

Go to school, go to school.

This is the way we go to school,

On a cold and frosty morning.

SUGGESTION: Children can sing this song and act it out very creatively, especially as a transition between activities. Make up your own verses: *this is the way we start the day, go to lunch, take a nap, read a book, tie our shoes,* and so forth. They can also change the song to suit the weather (*warm and sunny morning*).

This Is the Way We Wash Our Face

This is the way we wash our face,

Wash our face, wash our face,

This is the way we wash our face,

Until we're squeaky clean.

SUGGESTION: Have children sing this to the tune of "Here We Go 'Round the Mulberry Bush." Children may spontaneously mime washing their faces. Once they are familiar with the repetitive pattern, create new verses by substituting new body parts: *cheeks, ears, elbows, neck, hands*, etc. Also substitute other action words like *scrub, rub, dry*, and so forth. Explain the meaning of *squeaky clean*.

fold here

This Little Piggy

This little piggy went to market,

This little piggy stayed home,

This little piggy had roast beef,

This little piggy had none.

This little piggy went . . .

Wee, wee, wee,

All the way home!

SUGGESTION: Children may remember this rhyme from babyhood, when a loved one may have grabbed their toes while reciting the lines. With this in mind, invite children to use finger movements; starting with the little finger, ask them to wiggle each finger in succession and then wave the thumb while saying the last three lines. Let children replace *roast beef* with a favorite food of their own. Or have them substitute other animals and change the sound accordingly.

This Old Man

This old man, he played one,

He played knick-knack on his thumb;

With a knick-knack paddywhack, give your dog a bone,

This old man came rolling home.

ADDITIONAL VERSES:

two—shoe

three—knee

four—door

five—hive

six—sticks

seven—pen

eight—gate

nine—spine

ten—once again

May be photocopied for classroom use. ©2018 by Irene C. Fountas and Gay Su Pinnell from *Sing a Song of Poetry, Kindergarten*. Portsmouth, NH: Heinemann.

SUGGESTION: This oral-language counting song will help children think about number words and words that rhyme with them. You may want to have children hold up a large numeral and/or word card at the appropriate verse.

fold here

Three Blind Mice

Three blind mice,

See how they run!

See how they run!

They all ran after the farmer's wife,

Who cut off their tails with a carving knife;

Did you ever see such a sight in your life

As three blind mice?

May be photocopied for classroom use. ©2018 by Irene C. Fountas and Gay Su Pinnell from *Sing a Song of Poetry, Kindergarten*. Portsmouth, NH: Heinemann.

fold here

SUGGESTION: Teach children how to sing to the tune of this classic nursery rhyme. Then show them your favorite book adaptation of the poem to help reinforce its images. Invite children to substitute *blind* for different adjectives: e.g., color or size descriptors. The sillier the adjective, the sillier the sight!

Three Little Kittens

Three little kittens lost their mittens,
And they began to cry,
"Oh, Mother dear, we very much fear
Our mittens we have lost!"

"What, lost your mittens, you naughty kittens!
Then you shall have no pie."
"Meow, meow, meow, meow."
"No, you have shall have no pie."

The three little kittens found their mittens,
And they began to cry,
"Oh, Mother dear, see here, see here,
Our mittens we have found."

"What! Found your mittens? You good little kittens,
Now you shall have some pie."
"Purr, purr, purr, purr,
Purr, purr, purr."

SUGGESTION: Assign small groups of children to say the dialogue of the mother, the kittens, and the narrator. This poem lends itself to making a story map with pictures, one for each verse.

fold here

Three Men in a Tub

Rub-a-dub-dub,

Three men in a tub,

And who do you think were there?

The butcher, the baker,

The candlestick maker,

And all had come from the fair.

May be photocopied for classroom use. ©2018 by Irene C. Fountas and Gay Su Pinnell from *Sing a Song of Poetry, Kindergarten*. Portsmouth, NH: Heinemann.

fold here

SUGGESTION: Have a small group of children say *rub-a-dub-dub* while the rest read the rhyme. You may need to discuss the meaning of *butcher*, *baker*, and *candlestick maker*.

Time to Pick Up

Now it is time

To end our day.

Pick up our materials

And put them away.

SUGGESTION: Here is a rhyme to sing or say while cleaning the room. After learning this rhyme, invite children to say it with you as they clean up. Substitute more detailed words for *materials* like *blocks*, *puppets*, *crayons*, and *papers*.

fold here

A Tisket, a Tasket

A tisket, a tasket,

A green and yellow basket.

I wrote a letter to my friend

And on my way I lost it.

I lost it, I lost it,

And on the way I lost it.

A little child picked it up,

And put it in her pocket.

Her pocket, her pocket,

She put it in her pocket.

A little child picked it up,

And put it in her pocket.

May be photocopied for classroom use. ©2018 by Irene C. Fountas and Gay Su Pinnell from *Sing a Song of Poetry, Kindergarten.* Portsmouth, NH: Heinemann.

SUGGESTION: Have children play a game while reciting this rhyme. The child who is "it" skips around the outside of a circle of seated classmates while carrying a basketful of letters—pieces of paper with an easy word, a letter of the alphabet, or someone's name written on them. After the child who is "it" drops a letter behind another child, this chosen child jumps up, picks up the letter, runs after the basket carrier, and tries to tag him or her. If the attempt is successful, the second child is "it" and gets the basket. Substitute children's names for *my friend* and *a little child*.

To Market, to Market

To market, to market,

To buy a fat pig.

Home again, home again,

Jiggety jig.

ADDITIONAL VERSES:

To market, to market,

To buy a fat hog.

Home again, home again,

Jiggety jog.

SUGGESTION: Invite children to draw and dictate or write how they might go to market and what they might buy. Have them recite the verse in various configurations and jump up when they say the words *jiggety jig*.

May be photocopied for classroom use. ©2018 by Irene C. Fountas and Gay Su Pinnell from *Sing a Song of Poetry, Kindergarten*. Portsmouth, NH: Heinemann.

fold here

Today

Today is Monday, today is Monday,

How are you, how are you?

Very well, I thank you,

Very well, I thank you,

How about you? How about you?

May be photocopied for classroom use. ©2018 by Irene C. Fountas and Gay Su Pinnell from *Sing a Song of Poetry, Kindergarten*. Portsmouth, NH: Heinemann.

fold here

SUGGESTION: Have children sing this verse to the tune of "Are You Sleeping?" Assign some to read the first two lines and others to read the response. Substitute the other days of the week to create another six verses.

Tommy Snooks

As Tommy Snooks and Bessy Brooks

Were walking out one Sunday,

Said Tommy Snooks to Bessy Brooks,

"Tomorrow will be Monday."

SUGGESTION: You can substitute children's names for *Tommy Snooks* and *Bessy Brooks*. This simple rhyme will help children remember the sequence of days in the week. Looking at the calendar, start on any day and have children figure out what *tomorrow* would be.

fold here

Tommy Thumbs

Tommy Thumbs up and

Tommy Thumbs down.

Tommy Thumbs dancing

All around the town.

Dancing on my shoulders.

Dancing on my head.

Dancing on my knees.

Now, tuck them into bed.

ACTIONS:

Tommy Thumbs up and [*thumbs-up sign*]

Tommy Thumbs down. [*both thumbs down*]

Tommy Thumbs dancing

All around the town. [*make thumbs dance*]

Dancing on my shoulders. [*dance thumbs on shoulders*]

Dancing on my head. [*dance thumbs on head*]

Dancing on my knees. [*dance thumbs on knees*]

Now, tuck them into bed. [*fold arms, hiding hands*]

May be photocopied for classroom use. ©2018 by Irene C. Fountas and Gay Su Pinnell from *Sing a Song of Poetry, Kindergarten*. Portsmouth, NH: Heinemann.

fold here

SUGGESTION: Teach children to perform the accompanying actions. Repeat with the rest of the digits individually (*Peter Pointers, Toby Talls, Ringmen, Baby Fingers*) and then with all of them at once (*Finger Family*).

Toys Away

Toys away,

Toys away,

Time to put our

Toys away.

SUGGESTION: Have children chant this while they are putting things away. When appropriate, substitute other words for toys like *blocks*, *books*, and *coats*.

fold here

Twinkle, Twinkle, Little Star

Twinkle, twinkle, little star,

How I wonder what you are!

Up above the world so high,

Like a diamond in the sky.

Twinkle, twinkle, little star,

How I wonder what you are!

fold here

SUGGESTION: Have children sing the song. Substitute other words for *diamond* and illustrate the resulting poems with crayons. Together, create a new version of the poem using comical words and images like this classic one by Lewis Carroll from *Alice's Adventures in Wonderland*: *Twinkle, twinkle, little bat! / How I wonder what you're at! / Up above the world you fly, / Like a tea-tray in the sky. / Twinkle, twinkle, little bat! / How I wonder what you're at!*

Two, Four, Six, Eight

Two, four, six, eight,

Meet me at the garden gate.

If I'm late, do not wait,

Two, four, six, eight.

SUGGESTION: This rhyme has a strong beat. Have children use rhythm sticks or hand claps to mark each number word. After children have learned the rhyme, you may want to use a number line to show that they are skipping every other number.

fold here

Two Little Blackbirds

Two little blackbirds

Sitting on a hill,

One named Jack,

One named Jill.

Fly away, Jack,

Flay away, Jill.

Come back, Jack,

Come back, Jill.

ACTIONS:

Two little blackbirds [*both hands on shoulders*]

Sitting on a hill,

One named Jack, [*lift right hand above shoulder and put back down*]

One named Jill. [*lift left hand*]

Fly away, Jack, [*flutter right hand to reach up high*]

Fly away, Jill. [*flutter left hand to reach up high*]

Come back, Jack, [*bring right hand back to shoulder*]

Come back, Jill. [*bring left hand back to shoulder*]

May be photocopied for classroom use. ©2018 by Irene C. Fountas and Gay Su Pinnell from *Sing a Song of Poetry, Kindergarten*. Portsmouth, NH: Heinemann.

fold here

SUGGESTION: Perform this poem as a finger play or puppet show. Invite children to make little puppets by cutting out blackbirds from construction paper and attaching them to craft sticks.

Two Little Houses

Two little houses,

Closed up tight.

Let's open the windows,

And let in some light.

ACTIONS:

Two little houses, [*make two fists*]

Closed up tight.

Let's open the windows, [*stick thumbs out*]

And let in some light. [*open hands*]

SUGGESTION: This finger play is a good poem for shared reading. Create an enlarged version with two houses whose cut-out windows open and shut.

fold here

Up in the North

Up in the North, a long way off,

A donkey got the whooping cough;

He whooped so hard with the whooping cough,

He whooped his head and tail right off.

SUGGESTION: Explain the meaning of *whooped*. Children will find this poem funny once they realize that the donkey coughed its head and tail off. They can say the poem several times, substituting the names of different animals.

Up to the Ceiling

Up to the ceiling,
Down to the floor,
Left to the window,
Right to the door.

This is my right hand—
Raise it up high.
This is my left hand—
Reach for the sky.

Right hand, left hand,
Twirl them around.
Left hand, right hand,
Pound, pound, pound.

May be photocopied for classroom use. ©2018 by Irene C. Fountas and Gay Su Pinnell from *Sing a Song of Poetry, Kindergarten*. Portsmouth, NH: Heinemann.

SUGGESTION: This rhyme gives children a good stretch break between activities and lets them practice distinguishing the left and right hands. The hand actions, in order, are: raise hands up, put hands down, point left with the left hand, point right with the right hand, raise right hand, raise left hand while keeping right hand up, twirl hands one around the other, and hit fists together three times.

fold here

Wash Hands, Wash

Wash hands, wash,

Daddy's gone to plow.

If you want your hands washed,

Wash them now.

May be photocopied for classroom use. ©2018 by Irene C. Fountas and Gay Su Pinnell from *Sing a Song of Poetry, Kindergarten*. Portsmouth, NH: Heinemann.

VARIATION:

Warm hands, warm,

The men are gone to plow.

If you want to warm your hands,

Warm them now.

SUGGESTION: Assign half the children to read the first two lines and the other half to read the last two lines. You may need to discuss the meaning of *plow*.

We Can

We can jump, jump, jump,

We can hop, hop, hop,

We can clap, clap, clap,

We can stop, stop, stop.

We can nod our heads for yes,

We can shake our heads for no,

We can bend our knees a tiny bit,

And sit down very slow.

SUGGESTION: This is a good poem to use to help children move from one activity to another. Have them complete the actions as they say the words. Ask children to say the four words that end the lines in verse one. If they say them slowly, they can hear the /p/ at the end of each word. Create a print version of verse 1 and have children locate words that end in the letter *p*.

fold here

Wee Willie Winkie

Wee Willie Winkie runs through the town,

Upstairs, downstairs, in his nightgown;

Rapping at the window,

Crying at the lock,

"Are the children all in bed?

For now it's eight o'clock!"

SUGGESTION: Children are fascinated by the image of Wee Willie Winkie running through the streets to check that all children are in bed. Tell them about the days when lamplighters lit the streetlights at night. Substitute other times for *eight o'clock* and other names for *Wee Willie Winkie*. Children can say *Wee Willie Winkie* and notice that the words sound the same at the beginning.

What's the Weather?

What's the weather?

What's the weather?

What's the weather like today?

Is it rainy?

Is it windy?

Are there clouds or is there sun?

ADDITIONAL VERSES:

It is _____.

It is _____.

That's the weather today.

Today, it is _____.

It is _____ today.

May be photocopied for classroom use. ©2018 by Irene C. Fountas and Gay Su Pinnell from *Sing a Song of Poetry, Kindergarten*. Portsmouth, NH: Heinemann.

SUGGESTION: Sing this to the tune of "Oh, My Darling Clementine." Invite children to sing this in the morning while arriving as a way to react to the day's weather. Half the group can sing the question (which remains the same) while the other half sings the response (which changes with the weather).

fold here

The Wheels on the Bus

The wheels on the bus
Go 'round and 'round,
'Round and 'round,
'Round and 'round.
The wheels on the bus
Go 'round and 'round
All around the town.

ADDITIONAL VERSES:

The wipers on the bus
Go swish, swish, swish,
Swish, swish, swish,
Swish, swish, swish.
The wipers on the bus
Go swish, swish, swish
All around the town.

The people on the bus
Get up and down,
Up and down,
Up and down.
The people on the bus
Get up and down
All around the town.

The baby on the bus
Cries, "Wah, wah, wah"
"Wah, wah, wah"
"Wah, wah, wah."
The baby on the bus
Cries, "Wah, wah, wah"
All around the town.

The driver on the bus
Calls, "Move on back!"
"Move on back!"
"Move on back!"
The driver on the bus
Calls, "Move on back!"
All around the town.

The horn on the bus
Goes beep, beep, beep,
Beep, beep, beep,
Beep, beep, beep.
The horn on the bus
Goes beep, beep, beep,
All around the town

The parents on the bus
Go, "Shh, shh, shh,"
"Shh, shh, shh,"
"Shh, shh, shh."
The parents on the bus
Go, "Shh, shh, shh,"
All around the town.

May be photocopied for classroom use. ©2018 by Irene C. Fountas and Gay Su Pinnell from *Sing a Song of Poetry, Kindergarten*. Portsmouth, NH: Heinemann.

fold here

SUGGESTION: Children love pantomiming the motions and making representative onomatopoeic sounds as they sing or recite each verse. Help them create some new verses: e.g., *the lights go blink, blink, blink; the door goes open/shut*; and *the dogs go bark, bark, bark*. Mary Kovalski's *The Wheels on the Bus* (1991) extends the traditional song ideas to tell a different story. Lenny Hort's book, *The Seals on the Bus* (2000), is a humorous adaptation. Another humorous adaptation to read together is *The Wheels on the Bike* by Anne Stribling found in the *Fountas & Pinnell Classroom™ Shared Reading Collection, Kindergarten* (2018).

When Ducks Get Up
in the Morning

When ducks get up in the morning,

They always say, "Quack, Quack."

When ducks get up in the morning,

They always say, "Quack, quack.

Quack, quack, quack, quack, quack, quack."

They always say, "Quack, quack."

SUGGESTION: Substitute other animals and sounds to create more verses: *birds—tweet, tweet; cows—moo, moo; cats—meow, meow; dogs—bow-wow; sheep—baa, baa; pigs—oink, oink.*

fold here

Where Is Thumbkin?

Where is thumbkin?

Where is thumbkin?

Here I am.

Here I am.

How are you today, sir?

Very well, I thank you.

Run away.

Run away.

ACTIONS:

Where is thumbkin? [*hands behind back*]

Where is thumbkin?

Here I am. [*show one thumb*]

Here I am. [*show other thumb*]

How are you today, sir? [*bend one thumb toward the other*]

Very well, I thank you. [*bend opposite thumb in response, as if talking*]

Run away. [*return one thumb and hand behind back*]

Run away. [*return other thumb and hand behind back*]

May be photocopied for classroom use. ©2018 by Irene C. Fountas and Gay Su Pinnell from *Sing a Song of Poetry, Kindergarten.* Portsmouth. NH: Heinemann.

SUGGESTION: Sing this song to the tune of "Are You Sleeping?" Have children act out the whole story. Extend the rhyme by substituting all the other digits, one at a time: *Where is pointer? Tall one? Ring finger? Pinkie?* As a variation, have children sit in a circle. Substitute a child's name for *thumbkin* as you sing the first two lines. The named child sings lines 3 and 4; you sing line 5; and then the named child sings lines 6, 7, and 8 before beginning the verse again using a new child's name.

Who Is Wearing Red?

Oh, who is wearing red?

Oh, who is wearing red?

Please tell me if you can,

Oh, who is wearing red?

Oh, _____ is wearing red.

Oh, _____ is wearing red.

That's the color of her _____.

Oh, _____ is wearing red.

May be photocopied for classroom use. ©2018 by Irene C. Fountas and Gay Su Pinnell from *Sing a Song of Poetry, Kindergarten*. Portsmouth, NH: Heinemann.

fold here

SUGGESTION: The text can be sung to the tune of "The Farmer in the Dell." Invite the class to insert a child's name in the blank spaces after *Oh*, as well as the name of the article of clothing in the third line of response. Showing the words of this song in a pocket chart allows you to insert cards with alternative names and colors.

Who Stole the Cookies?

Who stole the cookies

from the cookie jar?

_____ stole the cookies

from the cookie jar.

Who, me?

Yes, you.

Couldn't be.

Then, who?

fold here

SUGGESTION: Use this rhyme to play a circle game, substituting different children's names each time. The child whose name is said aloud reads *Who me?* and *Couldn't be* and then starts the rhyme again by inserting a new child's name. Alternatively, hold up a name card instead of saying the name orally. Pair this poem with the picture book *Who Took the Cookies from the Cookie Jar?* by Bonnie Lass and Philemon Sturges (2000).

The Whole Duty of Children

by Robert Louis Stevenson

A child should always say what's true,

And speak when he is spoken to,

And behave mannerly at table:

At least as far as he is able.

SUGGESTION: Invite children to discuss what good manners are in your classroom. Turn the poem into a list through interactive writing (*tell the truth, listen and answer, clean up your materials*).

Whoops, Johnny

Johnny, Johnny, Johnny, Johnny,

Whoops, Johnny,

Whoops, Johnny,

Johnny, Johnny, Johnny, Johnny.

fold here

SUGGESTION: Make a game out of this poem. Invite children to say *Johnny* while using the index finger of the right hand to tap the top of each finger of the opposite hand—beginning with the pinky. Then direct them to slide the right index finger from the top of the left index finger down along the curve to the left pinky before tracing back to the top of the thumb. Have children repeat the action in reverse for the last two lines, and encourage them to substitute for *Johnny* with other children's names.

Why Rabbits Jump

"Why are you rabbits jumping so?

Now please tell why, tell why."

"We jump to see the big round moon

Up in the sky, the sky."

May be photocopied for classroom use. ©2018 by Irene C. Fountas and Gay Su Pinnell from *Sing a Song of Poetry, Kindergarten.* Portsmouth, NH: Heinemann.

SUGGESTION: Divide the class into two, and have half of the children read the first two lines and the others read the final two lines. Let one group be rabbits and jump every time they hear the word *jump*. Invite children to take turns being rabbits.

fold here

Willaby, Wallaby, Woo

Willaby, wallaby, woo,

An elephant stepped on you.

Willaby, wallaby, wee,

An elephant stepped on me.

SUGGESTION: Children love to act out this rhyme. Change *woo* to words that rhyme with children's names: *Willaby, wallaby, wason, / An elephant stepped on Jason; Willaby, wallaby, wackie, / An elephant stepped on Jackie*; and so forth. The sillier the rhymes, the more intriguing the verse.

Wind the Bobbin

Wind, wind, wind the bobbin,

Wind, wind, wind, the bobbin,

Pull, pull,

Clap! clap! clap!

ACTIONS:

Wind, wind, wind the bobbin, [*turn hands around*]

Wind, wind, wind, the bobbin, [*turn hands around*]

Pull, pull, [*pull hands from center out*]

Clap! clap! clap! [*clap three times*]

SUGGESTION: Discuss what a bobbin is and how it is used. Bring in a sewing machine bobbin for children to look at. Have them make winding hand motions as they say the poem.

fold here

Window Watching

See the window I have here,

So big and wide and square.

I can stand in front of it,

And see the things out there.

fold here

SUGGESTION: Invite children to add hand movements: draw a square in the air for lines 1 and 2, and shade the eyes as if looking in the distance for lines 3 and 4. After reciting the poem, ask children to draw themselves looking out the *big and wide and square* window at whatever their imagination comes up with. Have them label what they draw themselves seeing. Also, consider posting a copy of the poem next to a window in your classroom.

Windshield Wiper

I'm a windshield wiper.

This is how I go:

Back and forth, back and forth,

In the rain and snow.

SUGGESTION: Have children enact this poem by moving one or both arms as they chant: bend arm at elbow, fingers pointing up; move arm left and right, pivoting at the elbow. They can vary the tempo to indicate different kinds of weather. Feature the poem with a picture of windshield wipers on a poetry chart.

fold here

Yankee Doodle

Yankee Doodle came to town,

Riding on a pony;

He stuck a feather in his cap

And called it macaroni.

fold here

SUGGESTION: Invite children to act out this poem by galloping in place like a pony. Then, on the third line, have them pretend to stick a feather in their imaginary cap. Children may find it interesting that *macaroni* once referred to a person who was fashionable, stylish, or pretty rather than to a food.

Zoom, Zoom, Zoom

Zoom, zoom, zoom,

I'm going to the moon.

If you want to take a trip,

Climb aboard my rocket ship.

Zoom, zoom, zoom,

I'm going to the moon.

May be photocopied for classroom use. ©2018 by Irene C. Fountas and Gay Su Pinnell from *Sing a Song of Poetry, Kindergarten*. Portsmouth, NH: Heinemann.

ACTIONS:

Zoom, zoom, zoom, [*brush hands together in an upward motion*]

I'm going to the moon. [*brush hands together again, sending the top hand very high*]

If you want to take a trip,

Climb aboard my rocket ship. [*pantomime climbing a ladder*]

Zoom, zoom, zoom, [*brush hands together in an upward motion*]

I'm going to the moon. [*brush hands together again, sending the top hand very high*]

SUGGESTION: Have children make the suggested hand movements as they recite the poem. As an alternative, have one child sit in a row of chairs as you say the poem. At the end, he or she chooses a child to board the *rocket ship*. Ask children to repeat the poem again and again until four or five children have been added.

fold here

References

Adams, Pam. 1977. *This Is the House That Jack Built.* Swindon, England: Child's Play. From *Fountas & Pinnell Classroom™ Interactive Read-Aloud Collection, Kindergarten.* © 2018 by Irene C. Fountas and Gay Su Pinnell. Portsmouth, NH: Heinemann.

Brown, Margaret Wise. 1977. *Two Little Trains.* New York, NY: HarperTrophy, an imprint of HarperCollins Publishers.

Cabrera, Jane. 2000. *Cat's Colors.* New York, NY: Puffin Books, an imprint of Penguin Young Readers Group, Penguin Random House. From *Fountas & Pinnell Classroom™ Interactive Read-Aloud Collection, Kindergarten.* © 2018 by Irene C. Fountas and Gay Su Pinnell. Portsmouth, NH: Heinemann.

Carle, Eric. 1977. *The Grouchy Ladybug.* New York, NY: HarperFestival, an imprint of HarperCollins Publishers.

Carroll, Lewis. 1865. *Alice's Adventures in Wonderland.* London, England: Macmillan Children's Books, an imprint of Macmillan Publishers.

Crews, Donald. 1978. *Freight Train.* New York, NY: Greenwillow Books, an imprint of HarperCollins Publishers.

dePaola, Tomie. 1978. *Pancakes for Breakfast.* Boston, MA: Houghton Mifflin Harcourt.

Dodd, Emma. 2003. *Dog's Colorful Day: A Messy Story about Colors and Counting.* New York, NY: Puffin Books, an imprint of Penguin Young Readers Group, Penguin Random House. From *Fountas & Pinnell Classroom™ Interactive Read-Aloud Collection, Kindergarten.* © 2018 by Irene C. Fountas and Gay Su Pinnell. Portsmouth, NH: Heinemann.

Eagle, Kin. 1994. *It's Raining, It's Pouring.* Watertown, MA: Charlesbridge. From *Fountas & Pinnell Classroom™ Interactive Read-Aloud Collection, Kindergarten.* © 2018 by Irene C. Fountas and Gay Su Pinnell. Portsmouth, NH: Heinemann.

Ehlert, Lois. 1997. *Hands.* Boston, MA: Houghton Mifflin Harcourt.

Fountas, Irene C. and Gay Su Pinnell. 2018. *Fountas & Pinnell Classroom™ Interactive Read-Aloud Collection, Kindergarten.* Portsmouth, NH: Heinemann.

———. 2018. *Fountas & Pinnell Classroom™ Shared Reading Collection, Kindergarten.* Portsmouth, NH: Heinemann.

———. 2018. *Fountas & Pinnell Phonics, Spelling, and Word Study Lessons, Kindergarten.* Portsmouth, NH: Heinemann.

———. 2017. *Guided Reading: Responsive Teaching Across the Grades,* Second Edition. Portsmouth, NH: Heinemann.

Galdone, Paul. 2001. *The Little Red Hen*. New York, NY: Houghton Mifflin Harcourt Books for Young Readers, an imprint of Houghton Mifflin Harcourt Books for Young Readers Division, Houghton Mifflin Harcourt. From *Fountas & Pinnell Classroom™ Interactive Read-Aloud Collection, Kindergarten*. © 2018 by Irene C. Fountas and Gay Su Pinnell. Portsmouth, NH: Heinemann.

Grimm, Jacob and Wilhelm Grimm. 2003. *The Elves and the Shoemaker*. San Francisco, CA: Chronicle Books.

Hoberman, Mary Ann and Nadine Bernard Westcott. 2004. *The Eensy-Weensy Spider*. New York, NY: Little, Brown Books for Young Readers, an imprint of Hachette Book Group. From *Fountas & Pinnell Classroom™ Interactive Read-Aloud Collection, Kindergarten*. © 2018 by Irene C. Fountas and Gay Su Pinnell. Portsmouth, NH: Heinemann.

Hort, Lenny. 2000. *The Seals on the Bus*. New York, NY: Henry Holt and Company, an imprint of Macmillan Publishers.

Hutchins, Pat. 1993. *Titch*. New York, NY: Aladdin, an imprint of Simon & Schuster Children's Publishing, Simon & Schuster.

Kovalski, Maryann. 1991. *The Wheels on the Bus: An Adaptation of the Traditional Song*. London, England: Puffin Books, an imprint of Penguin Young Readers Group, Penguin Random House.

Kraus, Robert. 1971. *Leo the Late Bloomer*. New York, NY: Windmill Books, HarperCollins Children's Book, a division of HarperCollins Publishers. From *Fountas & Pinnell Classroom™ Interactive Read-Aloud Collection, Kindergarten*. © 2018 by Irene C. Fountas and Gay Su Pinnell. Portsmouth, NH: Heinemann.

Langstaff, John and Nancy. 1986. *Sally Go Round the Moon: Revels Songs and Singing Games for Young Children*. Watertown, MA: Revels Records.

Lass, Bonnie and Philemon Sturges. 2000. *Who Took the Cookies from the Cookie Jar?* New York, NY: Little, Brown Books for Young Readers, an imprint of Hachette Book Group.

Lopez, Lisa. *Old MacDonald*. From *Fountas & Pinnell Classroom™ Shared Reading Collection, Kindergarten*. © 2018 by Irene C. Fountas and Gay Su Pinnell. Portsmouth, NH: Heinemann.

McCarrier, Andrea, Gay Su Pinnell, and Irene C. Fountas. 2000. *Interactive Writing: How Language and Literacy Come Together, K–2*. Portsmouth, NH: Heinemann.

McMillan, Bruce. 1993. *Mouse Views*. New York, NY: Holiday House.

Ormerod, Jan. 1996. *Ms. MacDonald Has a Class*. Boston, MA: Clarion Books, an imprint of Houghton Mifflin Harcourt Books for Young Readers Division, Houghton Mifflin Harcourt.

Pinnell, Gay Su and Irene C. Fountas. 1998. *Word Matters: Teaching Phonics and Spelling in the Reading/Writing Classroom*. Portsmouth, NH: Heinemann.

Quinn, Irene. *Wheels on the Move*. From *Fountas & Pinnell Classroom™ Shared Reading Collection, Kindergarten*. © 2018 by Irene C. Fountas and Gay Su Pinnell. Portsmouth, NH: Heinemann.

Stribling, Anne. *The Wheels on the Bike*. From *Fountas & Pinnell Classroom™ Shared Reading Collection, Kindergarten*. © 2018 by Irene C. Fountas and Gay Su Pinnell. Portsmouth, NH: Heinemann.

Swinburne, Stephen R. 2002. *What Color Is Nature?* Honesdale, PA: Boyds Mills Press, division of Highlights for Children. From *Fountas & Pinnell Classroom™ Interactive Read-Aloud Collection, Kindergarten*. © 2018 by Irene C. Fountas and Gay Su Pinnell. Portsmouth, NH: Heinemann.

Thong, Roseanne. 2008. *Red Is a Dragon*. San Francisco, CA: Chronicle Books. From *Fountas & Pinnell Classroom™ Interactive Read-Aloud Collection, Kindergarten*. © 2018 by Irene C. Fountas and Gay Su Pinnell. Portsmouth, NH: Heinemann.

Trapani, Iza. 2001. *Baa Baa Black Sheep*. Watertown, MA: Charlesbridge. From *Fountas & Pinnell Classroom™ Interactive Read-Aloud Collection, Kindergarten*. © 2018 by Irene C. Fountas and Gay Su Pinnell. Portsmouth, NH: Heinemann.

Trapani, Iza. 1996. *I'm a Little Teapot*. Watertown, MA: Charlesbridge. From *Fountas & Pinnell Classroom™ Interactive Read-Aloud Collection, Kindergarten*. © 2018 by Irene C. Fountas and Gay Su Pinnell. Portsmouth, NH: Heinemann.

Wells, Rosemary. 1998. *The Bear Went over the Mountain*. New York, NY: Scholastic Press.